In the Shadow of Vietnam

In the Shadow of Vietnam

Essays, 1977–1991

W. D. EHRHART

McFarland & Company, Inc., Publishers

Jefferson, North Carolina, and London

Acknowledgments

The essays first appeared in the following publications: • "On the Death of Robert Lowell," *In These Times*, October 19–25, 1977. • "On Michael Herr's *Dispatches*," *WIN* magazine, May 18, 1978. • "Politics and Poetry in South Africa," *WIN* magazine, September 28, 1978. • "The Long Road Home to Intimacy," *WIN* magazine, March 1, 1980. • "An Address to Middle America," *Fourth Dimension*, June 1980. • "Places and Ways to Live," *Another Chicago Magazine*, no. 6, 1981 • "The United States Screw & Bolt Company," *National Vietnam Veterans Review*, v. 2, no. 4, May 1982. • "Learning the Hard Way," pamphlet from Central Committee for Conscientious Objectors, 1982. • "Waiting for the Fire," *Poetry East*, nos. 9 & 10, winter/spring, 1982/83. • "Preserving the American Myth," *Intervention*, v. 1, no 1, spring 1984. • "Going Back," *Philadelphia Inquirer Magazine*, March 16, 1986. • "Soldier-Poets of the Vietnam War," *The Virginia Quarterly Review*, v. 63, no. 2, spring 1987. • "Los Norteamericanos y Centroamérica," *Unwinding the Vietnam War*, The Real Comet Press, 1987. • "On Memorial Day," *USA Today*, May 22, 1987. • "On *The Genre of Silence*," *The Virginia Quarterly Review*, v. 65, no. 1, winter 1989. • "A Letter to McGeorge Bundy," *Present Tense*, v. 16, no. 6, September/October 1989. • "On Flag-Burning," *Philadelphia Inquirer*, October 25, 1989. • "Stealing Hubcaps," *Vietnam Generation*, v. 2, no. 1, 1990. • "Teaching the Vietnam War," *Joiner Center Newsletter*, The William Joiner Center, University of Massachusetts at Boston, v. 4, no. 1, July 1990. • "On U.S. Policy Toward Post-War Vietnam," *Indochina Newsletter*, no. 64, July–August 1990. • "Don't Stand on Protocol," *Gallery*, February 1991. • "Hue City Re-visited," *Gallery*, July 1991. • "A Common Language," *The Virginia Quarterly Review*, v. 67, no. 3, summer 1991.

LIBRARY OF CONGRESS CATALOGUING-IN-PUBLICATION DATA

Ehrhart, W.D. (William Daniel), 1948–
   In the shadow of Vietnam : Essays, 1977–1991 /
by W.D. Ehrhart.
      p.   cm.
   Includes index.

   ISBN 978-0-7864-6727-3
   softcover : 50# alkaline paper ∞

   1. Vietnamese Conflict, 1961–1975.   I. Title.
DS557.7.E45   2011
959.704'3—dc20   91-52508

BRITISH LIBRARY CATALOGUING DATA ARE AVAILABLE

Front cover design by David K. Landis (Shake It Loose Graphics)

Manufactured in the United States of America

McFarland & Company, Inc., Publishers
   Box 611, Jefferson, North Carolina 28640
   www.mcfarlandpub.com

For Anne

Woman with voice like a carillon
pealing the cold from my bones

and for Leela

And she sings,
not knowing she is singing
for a father much in need
of her partricular song

TABLE OF CONTENTS

PREFACE

I never intended to be a "Vietnam writer," and I have never thought of myself as a "Vietnam writer." That label has largely been imposed upon me by others. But it is also true, in looking at the body of my work, that nearly all of it in one way or another, directly or indirectly, as the essays contained in this book clearly demonstrate, has been informed by my irrevocable decision as a teenager to become a Marine and fight in Vietnam. And in fact, this is even more true than might be readily apparent. For better or worse, virtually everything I see, do and think is filtered through that seminal experience. Indeed, since I first contemplated joining the Marines in late 1965, my entire adult life has been lived in the shadow of Vietnam. Thus, this book contains essays on South Africa, Central America, early Soviet Russia, and contemporary flag-burning, along with the kinds of essays one might more readily expect to find in a book with such a title.

But my apparent obsession with Vietnam is not, I think, what it seems, regardless of what others might think. The war itself is history. Only one of the essays in this collection deals with the actual war itself, and it was written more than eleven years ago. Vietnam is of interest to me now, and this has been true for a very long time, only in so much as it informs the world I now live in and shapes the world my daughter and her peers will inherit. The Vietnam war was for me, finally, only a starting point, the door that opened into my own soul and pointed the way to a new understanding of myself, my country, and the community of nations.

Thus, "The United States Screw & Bolt Company" is an opportunity to consider why Ronald Reagan, who made movies in Hollywood during World War II, who staunchly supported the war in Vietnam while his own sons avoided military service, so willingly sent the Marines to Lebanon; why George Bush, whose sons did not serve in Vietnam or anywhere else that I know of, has twice put young Americans in harm's way in the space of less than a year; why Danforth Quayle, who spent the Vietnam war safe and snug in the National Guard, is now vice president of the United States.

Thus, "*Los Norteamericanos y Centroamérica*" is an opportunity to consider why we waged a brutally successful ten-year war on one of the poorest nations on earth and continue to spend $1.5 million a day on military aid to equally poor El Salvador while our own cities are overflowing with the homeless, our streets are overflowing with drugs, our forests and lakes are dying of acid rain, our healthcare system is out of control, and many if not most of our public schools are bankrupt, physically deadly environments where education in any meaningful sense has long since ceased.

Thus, "Preserving the American Myth" is an opportunity to consider what we believe about ourselves, why we believe it, and what it costs us to ignore reality; "On Michael Herr's *Dispatches*" is an opportunity to consider the deadly romance of war; "On *The Genre of Silence*" is an opportunity to consider the power of words; "Politics and Poetry in South Africa" is an opportunity to consider the consequences of hypocrisy; "On Flag-Burning" is an opportunity to consider how and why frivolous idiocies take the place of real debate in our society; and "An Address to Middle America" is an opportunity to consider the price of acquiescence.

For a long time, I have periodically tried to forget Vietnam, and when I could not, I felt, or was made to feel, as if there were something horribly wrong with me. But I have come to believe that those around me have wanted me to "forget Vietnam and get on with my life" because that is exactly what they want desperately to do, and what I write makes it difficult for them to do so. Vietnam raised all sorts of fundamental questions that Americans have only rarely had to face. It exposed a darker side of ourselves, our government and our society that we do not like to acknowledge, let alone deal with or answer for. It is easier to pretend that it never happened, or that the meddling politicians and hippies had not let the boys "fight to win," or that it was in Ronald Reagan's words "in truth a noble cause," or that it is just ossified and irrelevant history, having no bearing on the world we live in today.

But even as I write this, hundreds of thousands of U.S. soldiers are deployed in the sands of Saudi Arabia. In all probability, whatever is going to befall them will have happened long before what I am writing actually gets into print. I hope they all come home safely. There is nothing in that part of the world I want them to kill or to die for. I have no interests there, and neither do they.

But if we wake up from this nightmare before it turns deadly, if history is any guide, there will only be others waiting. Sooner or later, as has already happened nearly a dozen times just since the end of the war in Vietnam, young Americans will again return to our shores in body bags. And what will they have died for? What will our government tell their families and the rest of us? What will we believe? And what will be true?

The night before I left for Vietnam in 1967, I wrote a last letter to my parents, to be opened only if I were killed. This past summer, after my mother died, my father having died in 1988, I came upon the sealed letter among her papers. This is how it began: "I ask only that you do not grieve for my death. I do not grieve; you must not grieve either. I am only too glad and proud to have given my life for my country. Be proud that I died for my country. I am happy in death for I have been given the chance to die for a cause, the cause of freedom. Whether this war is wrong or right, I do not know. But my country is engaged in it, and I believe in my country, and so I am willing to die for these United States."

My parents never read those words. They got their son back alive — as well as two other sons who also served voluntarily in Vietnam. They were lucky, because I was only 17 and they had had to cosign for my life when I'd enlisted, and I think they came in later years to regret the trust they'd placed in our government and our leaders. I certainly have, and it embarrasses me to read those words now. How could I have been so naïve, so utterly trusting, so willing to offer up my life to men who would use it so callously? But that is why armies are always made of the young. It is not in the nature of youth to be wise or distrustful or selfish. And thus it is incumbent upon us, who know better, or ought to, not to ask for their lives unless it is absolutely and unavoidably necessary.

Was it absolutely and unavoidably necessary for those 287 Marines to die in Beirut? Or those 37 sailors in the Persian Gulf? Or those 23 soldiers in Panama City? Or those 58,000 men and women whose names are chiseled into that ugly black wall sunk into the earth on the mall of our nation's capital? Our government thinks so. Apparently a great many other Americans still think so, too. And if all the names of all the dead from the war in Indochina were carved into a wall, it would stand nine feet high and run from the Lincoln Memorial to the Washington Monument. I wonder what Abe and George would think about that.

We'll never know, of course, because the dead keep their thoughts to themselves, which is convenient because that way we never have to know what they think of the gassy rhetoric passing for patriotism that gets said over their graves. We never have to look them in the eye and explain what happened to our revolutionary heritage, or why we are continually fleeced, bamboozled and hoodwinked by a government that is supposed to be of the people, by the people and for the people. We can make up anything we want to, and believe it. It's a whole lot easier than trying to do something about it.

A Note on the Text

Of the twenty-three essays included in this book, nine originally appeared under different titles. Those titles were determined by the editors of the publications in which they appeared, not by me, and I have therefore replaced these externally imposed titles with titles of my own. In a few cases, I have reinserted material that was included in my original manuscripts but deleted by editors for reasons of space or whim. This is especially true of essays that originally appeared in daily newspapers.

Some of these essays have appeared in multiple versions. Where this has been the case, I have usually chosen to include the original version except where a later more complete version better reflects the manuscript version I wrote in the first place.

I have tried to keep actual revisions to a minimum, rewriting only when the original text demanded it for reasons of style or logic. I have made no attempt to update facts and references which are now, in some cases, five, ten, or even fourteen years out of date. While specific facts and references may thus be obsolete, the general sense of what I wrote in each essay still holds true.

W. D. Ehrhart
Fall 1990

ON THE DEATH
OF ROBERT LOWELL

In November 1967, while patrolling near Quang Tri, Vietnam, my squad came upon a batch of badly printed English-language leaflets, scattered by the Viet Cong. The leaflets, complete with photographs and quotes, told about the march on the Pentagon only a few weeks earlier. One of the names listed as having participated in the demonstration was Robert Lowell, the distinguished poet who died of a heart attack in New York in September 1977.

Nineteen years old, with five months still to serve in Vietnam and my whole world coming apart, I hated those leaflets. I hated Vietnam, and the Viet Cong and the demonstrators — including Robert Lowell. But I have learned a great deal in the last ten years, and one of the things I have learned is that Robert Lowell was a man to be respected, admired and thanked — and not just for the gift of his poetry.

One can hardly imagine a more unlikely political dissident than Lowell. Schooled at St. Mark's and Harvard, tutored by Richard Eberhart, Allen Tate and John Crowe Ransom, he was the inheritor of an aristocratic Puritan tradition stretching back to the *Mayflower*. Edward Winslow, Josiah Winslow, General John Stark, Amy Lowell, James Russell Lowell were his ancestors: ten generations of bankers and justices, academics and generals — Yankee bluebloods.

Lowell never got out from under the shadow of that past. Indeed, it was probably too vast for any human being to escape. But

1

he never felt fully comfortable with it, and his life was punctuated by remarkably independent actions.

Unhappy at Harvard, he transferred to Kenyon College in 1937. In 1940 he converted to Roman Catholicism. Though at the outbreak of World War II he unsuccessfully attempted to enlist in the navy (his father had been a career naval officer), by 1943 he had come to the conclusion that Allied bombing of civilian populations in Europe was morally indefensible. Denied conscientious objector status, Lowell was convicted of failure to obey the Selective Service Act and served four months in Danbury federal prison.

Later in the forties, with a growing reputation as a poet, Lowell was a member of the committee that awarded Ezra Pound the Bollingen Prize. Pound was not exactly popular at the time, and the decision required more than a little courage and integrity.

In 1965 Lowell refused Lyndon Johnson's invitation to a White House dinner, wiring that he regarded "our present foreign policy with dismay and distrust." He was the only major figure to decline that invitation. That was more than a year before I enlisted in the Marines.

Several years later, at the Ambassador Theatre in Washington, D.C., Lowell received a standing ovation for the poetry reading he had just given to a largely student antiwar audience. Leaving the stage, "Lowell did not seem particularly triumphant," wrote Norman Mailer in *Armies of the Night*. "He looked modest, still depressed, as if he had been applauded too much for too little."

The next day, Lowell was in the front rank of the marchers on their way to the Pentagon, matching strides with Benjamin Spock, Jerry Rubin and Dave Dellinger. Surely the staid patrician must have felt awkward in such company, alien even. But he was there.

None of this is to say that Lowell was a flaming radical, for certainly that was not the case. Not long before Lowell died, Louis Simpson, writing for the *Saturday Review*, correctly said of him that his "life has been much too sheltered. He has kept the best company, he has made his political protests under the best possible conditions.... He can have very little understanding of the kind of people who make up the mass—the poor and unlucky and obscure."

But to a sadly marked degree, most of us are the products of where we have come from. Within the terribly confining limits of his heritage, Lowell did what he could and at times when too few others were doing anything at all.

A few days after Lowell's death, I got a letter from Jan Barry, one of the founders of Vietnam Veterans Against the War. "Lowell I will always remember," he wrote, "not for a particular poem, but for quietly being there at so many peace demonstrations." Peace—

> After the planes unloaded, we fell down
> Buried together, unmarried men and women;
> Not crown of thorns, not iron, not Lombard crown,
> Not grilled and spindle spires pointing to heaven
> Could save us. Raise us, Mother, we fell down
> Here hugger-mugger in the jellied fire.
>   [from *The Dead in Europe*]

Most people will remember Robert Lowell for his poetry. But though I have come to admire his poems very much, I will remember Robert Lowell because, on a day when I hated him, he was trying to save my life.

ON MICHAEL HERR'S
Dispatches

The old mystique dies hard. Like some weird pied piper, the macho pride taught to young men before we reached the age of ten carried us off to Vietnam in search of our fathers' initiation into "manhood." It still rears its bloody head after all these years of nightmares and revelations.

Reading Michael Herr's *Dispatches*, I was astounded and demoralized to find myself bridling because Herr did not identify my battalion as the very first into the city of Hue during the 1968 Tet Offensive, angry because he did not say *why* Marines so disliked the 1st Air Cavalry Division, incensed because I disagreed with his assessment of the Marine Corps in Vietnam.

I spent an entire night lying awake after finishing the book, rethinking my whole experience and how I felt about it, reaffirming the convictions I hold against the madness of the culture we live in. Any book that can do that to me—and for me—has to have something going for it.

And *Dispatches* has a great deal going for it. Herr is a talented, indeed, brilliant writer. He kept his eyes open during his year in Vietnam as an *Esquire* correspondent, and his observations are often sensitive, painfully accurate, and deftly recorded. A word-photographer:

> [E]ven the most detailed maps didn't reveal much anymore; reading them was like trying to read the faces of the Vietnamese, and that was like trying to read the wind.

*   *

You could . . . fly out of places so grim they turned to black and white in your head five minutes after you'd gone.

* *

[E]verywhere you could smell that sour reek of obsolescence that followed the Marines all over Vietnam.

* *

We napalmed off [the Montagnards'] crops and flattened their villages, and then admired the restlessness in their spirit.

Dispatches is full of one- and two-liners like that that make you sit up and think, "Yeah, goddamn; yeah, that's just what it was like. Wow." Chilling, and powerful.

Equally remarkable are the vignettes of soldiers Herr weaves into a running commentary of his own. The "tunnel-rat" who, referring to General William Westmoreland and the light-at-the-end-of-the-tunnel, wondered: "What does that asshole know about tunnels?" The helicopter pilot "laughing and saying, 'Vietnam, man. Bomb 'em and feed 'em, bomb 'em and feed 'em.'" The courageous young Marine, having just saved his whole squad, unable to speak through his tears and sobbing.

Yes, this is a book which, as David Rabe says on the jacket notes, "gets very close to taking you all the way over"—until you put the book down, let it sit for awhile, and find yourself coming back repeatedly to a strange uneasiness inside, a feeling that something is very wrong with what you've just read. And you start trying to figure out why and what it is. And the more you think, the more "it" becomes a long, long list of "its."

Not long ago, I read one of Stephen Crane's dispatches from Cuba written during the Spanish-American War. In it, he praised the common soldiers, railed against the American people for failing to appreciate the brute courage and tremendous stoicism of these ordinary men, criticized the government for providing inadequate supplies and rotten food—and then blew it all by concluding that the Cuban soldiers [the ARVN of 1899] seemed curiously irresponsible and cowardly, and describing the largesse the United States was desirous of heaping upon insurgent [the VC of 1899] and "loyalist" alike.

Spanish Cuba was not Vietnam, and Michael Herr is not Stephen Crane. But the combination of poignant sympathy and wrongheaded blindness Crane possessed is uncannily reproduced by Herr. *Dispatches* is seldom ineffective in its verbal photography of war, even of the Vietnam war in particular. But Herr's conclusions are far too often wrong, superficial, or nonexistent.

Herr dwells obsessively on the soldiers' habit of collecting human ears (explicitly stating that half the troops in Vietnam engaged in such atrocities—a figure I find hard to believe, having spent thirteen months in an infantry battalion), while almost entirely missing far more hideous, if subtle brutalities. He portrays Westmoreland as the grotesque, blind idiot he was, but rarely mentions all the other grotesque, blind idiots who had as much of a hand in shaping American Indochina—most of whom Waste-More-Land took orders from, and many of whom still hold the reins of power.

Herr is eloquent in his identification with American "grunts," often eloquent in his lampooning of the military bureaucracy which "spoke goodworks and killed nobody," leaving the grunts to do the shit-work and carry the weight. But for all he says about the Vietnamese—ARVN, VC, NVA, or civilian—for most of the book you'd think there weren't any Vietnamese in Vietnam. They appear with few exceptions—when they appear—as cardboard cutouts, one-dimensional and voiceless.

At one point, during the battle for Hue, Herr says: "The bodies were stacked together and there was always a crowd of ARVN standing around staring, death-enthralled like all Vietnamese." What does he mean, "death-enthralled"? How does it differ from his own obvious enthrallment with death? What does he mean, "like all Vietnamese"? As opposed to whom? Americans? Penguins? The statement simply falls out onto the page, left to stand on its own with no further explanation, smacking of racism and profound ignorance.

Furthermore, while Herr apologizes and (perhaps) adequately explains why the *real* news of the war never reached the American people through the media establishment, the only real news Herr seems to have distills itself into Wilfred Owen's, "These men are worth your tears/You are not worth their merriment," or Rudyard Kipling's, "It's Tommy this and Tommy that...."

Most appalling, however, is Herr's delighted fascination with combat, with the exhilarating perpetually right-on-the-edge-of-death adrenalin life. It matters little that he readily admits that fascination: "All right, yes, it had been a groove being a war correspondent, hanging out with the grunts and getting close to the war, touching it, losing yourself in it and trying yourself against it. I had always wanted that, never mind why...."

Never mind why?! Yet that "why" lies at the very bottom of all those dead Americans stacked in huge green baggies he professes to urge the American people to weep for, all the maimed and emotionally damaged veterans walking around the streets of America and populating America's prisons, all the dead and displaced Vietnamese, the sickness infecting America and most of the rest of the world. Never mind why?

Moreover, while proclaiming disgust at the brutality of American soldiers, he claims that "I was in many ways brother to those poor, tired grunts, I knew what they knew now, I'd done it and it was really something." And this delivered with a straight face after stating earlier, "Sometimes you couldn't live with the terms any longer and headed for air conditioners in Danang and Saigon." Strange sense of brotherhood: if the "poor, tired grunts" couldn't live with the terms anymore, we had the choice of going to prison, going mad, or blowing off our own kneecaps.

Upon reflection, like the war itself, the list of troublesome items goes on and on. Like so many of us, Michael Herr went to Vietnam in search of his manhood. The really sad part is that he thinks he found it. For all the superficial differences, *Dispatches* is just another paean to men-at-war, a glorious-grisly-romantic tribute to the ultimate insanity. It is a tragic injustice to the men he so obviously loved and admired and pitied, for in its stock portrayal of war, it does its part to ensure that there will always be young men stacked in body-bags waiting to come home.

Perhaps if Herr had gone to Vietnam with a rifle instead of a notepad, he would have written a very different book. As it is, for all the book's excellent insights, polish, and virtues, young readers of *Dispatches* will not say "No More War," but only: "I hope my war isn't as stupid and senseless as Vietnam." The old mystique dies hard.

POLITICS AND POETRY
IN SOUTH AFRICA

Things are bad in apartheid South Africa. Everybody knows that. We deplore the situation; we wish it were not so, and hope it will change. But what can we do about it? Especially with all the injustices closer to home which command what little time and energy we have.

I recently received a letter from President Theodore Friend of Swarthmore College, of which I am an alumnus. In it, he invoked the "spirit of Quakerism" in criticizing the racist policies of the Republic of South Africa. But in a remarkable display of circle-talk newspeak, he said essentially that it would be fiscally imprudent for the college to divest itself of stock in companies with holdings in South Africa.

A few days later, a friend of mine gave me a copy of *Poets to the People* (Allen & Unwin, London), an anthology edited by Barry Feinberg of ten black South African poets, all of whom have been detained, imprisoned, tortured, or otherwise harassed by the white government, nine of whom now live in forced exile. Time and again, Friend's careful, diplomatic words returned to me as I read these poems:

> how long, oh how much longer must it be?
> how long still the wrench at throat
> the pluck at eyes
> at mention of some small forgotten word —
> Fietas or Woodstock or Gelvandale —?
> how much longer must we doggedly importune
> in the anterooms of governors of the world

or huddle stubborn on the draughty frontiers
    of strange lands?
how long must we endure?
        —Dennis Brutus

Once a volunteer under Gandhian colours,
head bleeding from double bludgeon
for turning cheek to set right thinking.
Then haunted by post-midnight squads,
splintered doors, splattered walls,
kicks and children clinging.
Years of guards beating in bleak yards,
conscience brothers thinned and shaking,
some, green on electric charges,
another, crazy dangled by borrowed belt.
        —Barry Feinberg

Day after day we [kindle] the fire,
Spreading the flame of our anger
Round your cities,
Round your children,
Who will remain the ash-monuments
Witnessing the explosions of our revenge.
        —Mazisi Kunene

The rage and suffering so eloquently and accurately conveyed in these poems underlined the hypocrisy and cowardice of that fund-raising letter from my old alma mater.

Black Voices Shout! (Troubadour Press, Chicago) is, if anything, even more insistent. Also poetry by black South Africans, it differs in several significant ways from *Poets to the People*. With the exception of James Matthews (editor of this anthology) and Mangone Wally Serote (who appears in both volumes), these poets are of a younger generation. All of them except Serote, who has gone into exile since the book's publication, are still living in South Africa. (Some of these nine poets too, needless to say, have been or are still in prison.)

The mechanics of this poetry are not as skillful as the poems in *Poets to the People,* but their naked straightforwardness actually adds to their impact. The anger of the poetry, to the exclusion of almost any other emotion, is frightening—perhaps reflecting the ever-increasing tension in South Africa, the immediacy of still living under the jackboot of apartheid:

I'll show you
Rats crawling around

Digesting our ghettos
Go black boy, uproot what you know and seek what's new....
Survival of the fittest was never a human principle.
                    —Christine Douts

I own dogs which I do not feed and when I sleep I
    chase the cats out
the flies the ants the rats the cockroaches in my house
    know
I pour boiling water on them and whistle a hymn....
I can sit opposite God and he will never be able to look
    me in the eye.
                    —Mangone Wally Serote

you want
me to remain the same as ever
obedient and meek
what then
if the wind blows away
your dream?
                    —Mike Dues

A child I am
of guns and grenades
'cause this will mean my liberty.
                    —Ilva Mackay

We'll pollute your white air
With Black Fury
Till it's filled
To the brim
Then
White South Africa
We'll come down
As an epidemic
Of Black
Freedom hunters.
                    —Steven Smith

Both anthologies, singly and together, strike like hammers on a cold steel anvil: prison, torture, "accidental" death while in police custody, families separated, segregated townships, travel passes, poverty, alcoholism, and rage; rage, rage—the recognition by these poets that only force of arms will free their people. The suggestion that real change might come without violence is almost nonexistent. One must turn to Dennis Brutus's *Strains* (Troubadour Press) to find even a crack in their rage:

> close your hand around time
> and my labouring intransigent heart
> and swear
> swear you forgive the world
> and the wry tangle of circumstance
> and pledge your commitment
> to sad, fumbling humanity.

It is amazing that Brutus can write such lines, for black South Africans surely have little reason to feel any commitment to any humanity beyond themselves and their people. Undoubtedly, all that keeps South Africa from becoming an open battlefield is the overwhelming military power of the white racist government. But it is only a matter of time.

Yet within that slight pause in the inevitable course of events, there is still the possibility of realizing nonviolent change in South Africa — though it is a very slim chance indeed, and it requires that a great many people bring to bear a great deal of pressure upon the apartheid government, upon our own and other governments, and upon the institutions and businesses which, actively or passively, directly and indirectly, support the present South African government.

The poems in *Poets to the People, Black Voices Shout!*, and *Strains* are an indictment of the white Western world, our complacence and our complicity. To continue to think in terms of fiscal security, prudent caution, and preservation of institutions is criminal. It is time to think about people — and as these poems so powerfully demonstrate, time is rapidly running out.

THE LONG ROAD
HOME TO INTIMACY

For a Sister of Mercy (1970)

Those were unsettling times —
surely no time to pity a man
trapped in a loaded barrel:
there were too many fires burning,
too many hammers waiting to fall;
all those angry people in the streets,
all those reasons why,
those questions, and broken dreams.

I did love you
in spite of all my solitary explorations,
that vast wound, some other life
I could not share
except in pain.

You were kind.
I am sorry I healed so slowly.
There was no other way.

I think of you often.

And I do think of that woman often. We were both young,
both first-year college students, both for the first time discovering
the depth and awesome beauty physical love can add to a relationship. It should have been a time of blossoming joy and
sharing.

But I was 21, an ex–Marine sergeant only recently removed from
an experience that had turned me inside out, at odds with my peers
at a small, politically active Quaker school where one couldn't be

just an anonymous face in the crowd, where people asked me constantly, "What was it like? Did you really kill anyone?"

I could barely keep the lid on the welter of emotions boiling inside of me, much less begin to try to sort it all out. Yet to most people I appeared calm, quiet and together: a man who'd been to the edge and come back, and couldn't be ruffled anymore by the mundane concerns of ordinary lives. People really believed that. My girlfriend certainly did. I think I did too, for awhile.

The pressure I was under, however, couldn't be checked forever. And ironically, as my girlfriend and I became closer, I began increasingly to vent my pent-up emotions on her. The woman I loved, who loved me, became the dumping ground for all the rage and confusion and shame locked inside of me. My behavior toward her became increasingly irrational—tyrannical fits of anger followed by weeping apologies begging forgiveness.

One day, in a rage prompted by some small thing I can't even recall, I struck my girlfriend with a closed fist, and with all my might. The silence that followed has never quite been completely dispelled. As I watched her cower in abject terror of me, I saw myself for the first time as I really was (and maybe still am somewhere deep inside). There was no rifle, no uniform, no officer giving orders under penalty of prison, no momentum of a vast organization. Yet her eyes were the same eyes I'd seen on a thousand faces in a hundred villages in Vietnam staring up at me in mute hatred as I stood over that bed, my whole body still cocked like a loaded pistol.

All the excuses I'd constructed for why I'd gone to Vietnam and what I'd done there came tinkling down around me, through that silence, like broken glass.

Though our relationship limped on for a few more months, I'm certain that was the day she made up her mind to get out. Eight years later, I'm still sorry. But if it was a terrible lesson to learn at a terrible price, it was also a turning point. From that moment on, I knew I would have to stop trying to hide, and deal head-on with my experience in Vietnam, and with myself.

Yes, I had reasons for being a walking powderkeg. I had had what at the time seemed plausible reasons for going to Vietnam. And there were even plausible reasons why that young woman had to suffer what she did. But reasons don't equal excuses. And violence, I had at last to recognize, isn't bounded by governments or soldiers, or rifles or knives or fists. Violence is a state of mind.

I've done pretty well since then. I haven't closed my fist on anyone in years, let alone on a woman I love. I get angry, of course, but I work consciously at dissipating it in other ways. But the fact remains that that first post–Vietnam love affair was the longest sustained relationship I've ever had—six months. I've known other women longer, dated other women and loved other women. But I've never lived with any of them, never opened my life quite so fully. And only the bravest of them—or the most blind—have ever asked me to.

So what? Maybe I'm just a little weird. Maybe I wasn't properly toilet trained. Maybe I just haven't bumped into a woman on the right wavelength. Vietnam veterans constantly run the risk of blaming the war for all our subsequent personal troubles. It's a compelling crutch, and readily available. Yet while we can't blame the war for an awkward date or a broken affair, the experience did change many of us, left scars that still linger.

Just what it affects, and how and how much, is hard to say—and surely must vary from vet to vet. Moreover, the effects aren't limited to romantic love (or whatever one wants to call it), but touch also relationships with friends, families and co-workers. One can "put the face on" for those one deals with sporadically, however, and they can easily ignore or tolerate private peeves. The intensity of a shared life precludes both these safety valves. Thus, if there are problems at all, they will manifest themselves most forcibly in that situation.

I think a major difficulty was and is a tremendous loss of self-confidence and self-esteem. Many veterans, whatever their private reasons for going, really believed at the outset in the essential rightness of what we were doing. That I could have been so wrong, with such lethal consequences, is staggering. It is hard to think well of oneself, knowing what one is capable of and, indeed, what one has done and been a part of. No amount of good ever makes up for it. Every moment of joy is shadowed by the knowledge that people who knew the same joys are dead because of me.

Am I too hard on myself? Self-pity is terribly destructive. And after awhile, people get fed up with it: "Let it go and get on with living." Therein lies another problem. A woman friend of mine said in a letter last year that she didn't like to hear about the war, or think about it, because it only upset her. But for many of us who were there, the nightmares don't stop because we say, "Stop."

The memories aren't self-destructing in five seconds, or ten years. In the same letter, in an entirely different context, my friend asked me why I always seemed on guard, as though I were constantly holding something back. I tried to explain, in the context of her own comments about the war. I haven't heard from her since. I suppose she had an exceptionally low tolerance level; I don't know. Yet whether my guilt is justified or not, in any close relationship, *both* parties are going to have to deal with it.

Any woman who chooses to deal with me is also going to have to deal with a palpable bitterness and cynicism, a slow-burning kind of rage. Once committed, I threw myself into the antiwar movement with a messianic passion, rightly or wrongly trying to use the movement to bring some good, some positive change out of what I had been through.

It was a simplistic drive for immediate results based on perhaps unachievable ideals. But instead of what I (and so many others) hoped for, we got the painfully slow withdrawal of ground troops, the vicious acceleration of the air war, the false peace, the babylift, the criminal mismanagement of the final evacuations, the half-assed amnesty years too late, the near-total amnesia of a nation.

Every disappointment deepened the bitterness, solidified the sense that we veterans were suckers, plain and simple, and nothing would ever mitigate that. It makes it hard ever to put one's faith and energies into anything again. And it's difficult to deal with a person who is cynical about almost everything almost all of the time.

But perhaps the biggest problem is not with other people — women in particular — trying to deal with us, but with our reluctance to share with women. I think it comes back to a feeling that I am, somewhere deep inside, essentially a bad person. Certainly I must be to do what I did — a convoluted but insistent logic. Therefore, if a woman gets to know me well enough, eventually she'll discover what I already know about myself — whereupon she'll reject me. But if I don't allow myself to get too close, I won't be left staring at myself in the mirror with all those unanswerable questions.

From what I can gather from friends, I'm not the only veteran whose first post–Vietnam love affair ended in disaster. To be rejected (even with good reason — perhaps worse because of it) at a time when one was so vulnerable reinforced from the start the questionable opinions one had of oneself, the sense of distrust.

I have already sounded a cautionary warning about the difficulties of assessing just what is responsible for what. Everything I've said here may well be false—and has certainly been oversimplified in any case. It is equally important to remember that I am attempting here to deal on a conscious level with effects which, if they function at all, operate on a far deeper and more subtle plane. And perhaps this article should be written, or at least coauthored, by the women who have loved me.

And there have been a few. I am neither a recluse nor an emotional basket case. Most Vietnam veterans aren't. And most of us have had, have now, or will have healthy, close, two-way relationships with women.

Furthermore, just about everyone I know has some kind of problem, some special demon or quirk or flaw to wrestle with. The kinds of problems I've tried to suggest here certainly aren't unique, though the circumstances causing them may be. And they aren't difficulties which are unmanageable.

They are real problems though, I think, however ill-defined and hard to disentangle from the web of influences which make all of us—men and women—distinct individuals. But if I want my lover to be sensitive to and supportive of me, I in turn must teach myself to be sensitive and supportive of her. Vietnam veterans, after all, aren't the only bunch that have gotten a bad rap to deal with.

AN ADDRESS TO
MIDDLE AMERICA

In the fall of 1976, I visited a journalism class at Pennridge High School in Perkasie, Pennsylvania, to talk about the Vietnam war. The first question I was asked was whether or not the antiwar movement in the United States had affected my morale while I was fighting in Vietnam.

I told the students that it had not, though we could not help being aware of the demonstrations. What had damaged my morale, I told them, was the discovery that the people we had been sent to defend did not want us there — and indeed, more often than not and with good reason, hated us; that we had been ordered by our government to win the hearts and minds of the people of Vietnam with nothing but rifles and bombs and American arrogance; that what we were involved in had nothing to do with the cause of freedom and democracy and liberty for which I had enlisted in 1966 at the age of 17; that we were Redcoats, not patriots, and that our national leaders had put us up to it; that we were killing and dying for something worse than nothing.

My answer fell on blank faces. After class was dismissed, the teacher who had invited me said that the kids had never heard anything like what I had said, that they were being taught in history class that the United States lost the war in Vietnam because the antiwar movement had undermined the morale of the troops and

Originally given as a speech to the members of Pebble Hill Church, Doylestown, Pennsylvania, June 1, 1980.

17

broken their will to win. The silence of the students, he said, was the silence of confusion and disbelief.

In 1977, I taught at the University of Illinois at Chicago. One day I happened to mention Dean Rusk. Again, silence. I asked the class of twenty-two college first- and second-year students who Dean Rusk was. Not only could no one tell me — none of them had ever heard the name.

In 1978, I taught at a Quaker high school in Maryland. In one class, we were studying the poet Philip Appleman, and I assigned five of Appleman's poems dealing with Vietnam. The next day, 16-year-old Liza Feeney began the class by asking, "Do we have to talk about this stuff?"

"Why don't you want to talk about it, Liza?" I asked.

"It's so depressing," she replied. "Why can't we talk about his love poems? They make me feel good."

"Do you know what happened in Vietnam?" I asked.

"We lost a war," she responded hesitantly. It was almost a question.

"What do you mean?" I asked. She shook her head slowly. She didn't have anything else she could add. Clearly, the only thought she could address the question with was the burning desire to have had the sense to keep her mouth shut in the first place.

"Do you know where Vietnam is, Liza?"

After a pause, she replied, "Somewhere in Asia, I think. Isn't it?"

Last fall, I went to a Vanderbilt–Air Force Academy football game. At halftime, a group of cadets came onto the field with an effigy of the Ayatollah Khomeini hanging from a pole and a large banner reading "Nuke Iran." They were clearly having a good time.

It's eerie. It is awesome and frightening. It is 1984 four years ahead of schedule. It is as though the events of the past fifteen years never happened. A catastrophic event that bent my life 180 degrees, a crime so grotesque I had thought the flag-waving myth of Duty-Honor-Country could never again be resurrected from its well-deserved grave, is as remote and irrelevant to the newest generation of potential cannon-fodder as are the civilizations of ancient Crete and Mycenae.

Is it possible that we have learned absolutely nothing? Is it even within the realm of imagination that we could so desecrate the memories of Khe Sanh and My Lai and Con Thien and Kent State and Jackson and Chicago? Are we really willing to allow another generation of children to march to their deaths for the pride of powerful men and the dividends of IBM and Exxon and Gulf & Western and Transamerica and Lockheed and Dow and Dupont?

And yet our children are ignorant. They know only what they have been taught — at home, in school, in the newspapers, on television, in church, at Boy Scouts and Girl Scouts, and the thousand other places and ways I learned the pigeon-breasted fantasies that filled my head the day I took the Oath of Allegiance and joined the United States Marine Corps thinking my sacrifice was a glorious gesture overflowing with grandeur and nobility.

We have taught our children nothing. We have wrapped ourselves in the shame of our complicity and the pain of our own shattered illusions and the fear of reprobation from our neighbors and friends and colleagues and associates, and allowed our children's perceptions of the world to be dictated by *The Deer Hunter* and *The Daily Intelligencer* and the press releases of Jody Powell.

Secretary of Defense Harold Brown catalogues the list of Russian evils in Afghanistan: helicopter gunships, wholesale search and seizure, napalm, aerial gas — and it's like hearing a recap of American Indochina — and he insists that such atrocities cannot be tolerated by a peace-loving American people. The same Harold Brown who was Secretary of the Air Force during the war in Vietnam. And we remain silent.

For humanitarian reasons, Jimmy Carter invites a broker of misery and oppression — a billionaire with a fortune built out of his people's blood and our tax dollars — to come to an American hospital, and when the people of Iran get angry, Carter expresses astonishment and outrage, exhorting his subjects to rally round the flag. And we remain silent.

The Defense Department is about to construct a nuclear shell-game in the deserts of Nevada and Utah in the form of the $17 billion MX Missile System while the food stamp program limps precariously from month to month and the price of hamburger soars to over $1.50 a pound and our schools — already overcrowded and understaffed — teeter on the brink of bankruptcy. And we remain silent.

Our own representative in Congress, Peter H. Kostmayer, says, "Clearly we have to take a strong stand against the Soviet invasion of Afghanistan" and "fully support" the Olympic boycott and a "5.2 percent increase above inflation" in the 1981 defense budget, stating that we must "demonstrate to the Soviets that we mean to protect our interests overseas." And we remain silent.

Has anybody asked himself or herself lately whose interests overseas are going to be protected? Has anybody asked lately, when the draft notices begin arriving in the mail—and they will begin arriving, whether it be next week or next month or next year—who will be ordered to protect those interests?

I can tell you who. Not the children of Robert McNamara, who is now president of the World Bank. Not the children of Dean Rusk, who is now Silbey Professor of International Law at the University of Georgia. Not the children of Clark Clifford, who is now a director of Phillips Petroleum Company. Not the children of McGeorge Bundy, who is now president of the Ford Foundation. Not the children of Harold Brown or Edmund Muskie or Jimmy Carter or Ronald Reagan or Edward Kennedy.

Our children are going to be ordered to protect those interests, that's who. Your children and my children. And the interests they will be fighting and killing and dying for won't be yours or mine or theirs.

And what have we given our children with which they might defend themselves against the stirring false words and shining false values utterly believed by false men and women who would make of a nation born of revolution and liberty a nation of sheep and followers?

Can we really afford to remain silent? Do we care so little for the next generation, and the one after that, and the one after that? Does it really cost more than we are willing to bear to teach our children the truth? Real patriotism often requires sacrifices greater than blood and obedience, and real love knows no price too high.

"Are you now contented to let . . . dissembling, insinuating men . . . carry their point against you, when you can, with infinitely more ease and safety, counterwork them. . .?" asked Christopher Gadsden, organizer of South Carolina's Sons of Liberty, in 1769. "Only be roused from your sleep; dare to see the truth, to support the truth; and the God of Truth will make you free."

And if we fail to dare, who will wear the shackles of our failure?

PLACES AND WAYS TO LIVE

Undoubtedly, the most useless piece of equipment issued by the United States Marine Corps in Vietnam was the shelter half. A holdover from the War of 1812, this was a heavy piece of canvas shaped to form one half of a small field tent commonly known as a pup tent. Along with the shelter half, you were issued half the total number of pegs needed for the whole tent, one of the two necessary poles (which came apart into three sections when not in use), and one of the two necessary support ropes. Some of the shelter halves had buttons along the seam that connected to the other half; others had buttonholes. Every Marine learned in boot camp the proper step-by-step procedure for constructing the tent.

However, unless you were willing to settle for half a tent (which is silly), in order to construct the tent successfully, you needed to find someone who fit all of the following requirements: he had to have a shelter half that was the opposite of yours (that is, if yours had buttons, his had to have buttonholes, and vice versa); he had to possess his full complement of pegs, pole sections and rope; he had to be able to remember the proper step-by-step procedure he'd learned in boot camp; and he had to be someone with whom you did not mind sleeping at close proximity.

If you actually managed to find someone who filled all of these requirements, and the two of you succeeded in getting your tent constructed before the sun rose and you had to pack up and leave again, you still had problems. The heavy canvas material rapidly caused the air inside the tent to become uncomfortably hot and stagnant. If the weather was good enough to enable you to open the end flap and let in fresh air, then you didn't need the tent in

21

the first place. And if it was raining, you couldn't open the flap because you would get wet. In addition, to say that the tent held two people is very much like those pudding mixes that say, "Makes four generous servings." (People in 1812 weren't as big as people are now. I went to Mount Vernon once and saw George Washington's bed; it was very small.) Moreover, if your body happened to touch the canvas while it was raining, which was impossible to prevent in the small confines of the tent, no matter how close you slept to your buddy, the waterproof seal on the canvas would be broken and the tent would leak for the rest of the night. Furthermore, the tent often fell down in the middle of the night because of faulty construction or the inability of the sandy soil in Vietnam to hold the short tent pegs under the strain caused by the weight of the heavy canvas. Finally, when not in use, the shelter half and its accessories were a cumbersome extra weight to be lugged around — a consideration worthy of the highest respect by all sensible infantrymen.

I threw my shelter half away at the earliest opportunity. So did nearly everyone else. One always tried to stay as far away as possible from anyone with a shelter half, for it was widely believed that anyone who lacked the sense to get rid of his shelter half would sooner or later manage to get you killed, though I don't believe the connection was ever actually proven since no one kept statistics on this, fond as the Pentagon was of numbers.

All sensible grunts carried ponchos instead of shelter halves. These were also useless for the purpose for which they were designed — that is, to be worn while walking in the rain — since the poncho covered everything you were carrying with many folds of loose material, and made access to things like ammunition and grenades extremely difficult in emergencies. Rain suits were much better because they kept you dry and alive at the same time. These were just rubberized pants and pullover shirts with hoods that were worn over your utility uniform but under your equipment. They were in short supply in the Marine Corps (as were all useful things), but you could always barter them off the Navy Seabees (Construction Battalion) or the Air Force for a disarmed Chinese grenade or an authentic Viet Cong battle flag made by one of the local tailors.

The poncho, however, was useful as a ground cloth when there was no need for a tent, which was the case during most of the dry season from April to September. And during the monsoons, the poncho became worth its weight in letters from home, for it made an easily constructed, remarkably efficient one-man tent.

To make a one-man poncho tent, you needed only your poncho, four little sticks, one stick about two feet long, and a bit of string (which usually came attached to the poncho). First, you pulled the drawstring tight on the face hole. Then you laid the poncho out in a loose rectangle on a flat bit of ground, and staked down the four corners with the little sticks. Then you reached inside with the long stick, poked it up into the poncho hood, and stood the stick upright, which would lift the poncho up from the center and stretch it into a taut, four-sided pyramid. Finally, you took the string and ran it from the center grommet on one side of the poncho to a nearby tree, bush or tank at about knee height in order to form a little entrance to the tent. If you wanted to get fancy, you could throw in a little brush or some banana leaves for a mattress. You were then ready to crawl in, curl up around the center pole, and go to sleep.

The one-man poncho tent took about three minutes to construct, almost never fell down because of its light weight and low profile, was fully waterproof because it was made of rubber rather than canvas, allowed ventilation in the rain, could be constructed even in the dark without assistance, and permitted you to sleep in privacy.

Furthermore, since it took so little time to construct, and demanded no time at all to locate a buddy who fulfilled all of the requirements for constructing a proper pup tent, the one-man poncho tent allowed you more time to spend digging your fighting hole. Every night you spent in the field, you had to dig a fighting hole with your entrenching tool. If you were on an operation and slept fifteen different places on fifteen different nights, you dug fifteen different fighting holes. Some nights you'd think, "Shit, I been walking all day; I'm too tired to dig." Then Tinney would remind you what Sullivan looked like after the mortar round landed next to him the night he'd been too tired. And when you thought about it, you were never really too tired to dig a fighting hole.

It didn't have to be anything grandiose — just enough to get you below ground level so that shrapnel from incoming mortar rounds and grenades would go over you instead of through you, and to give you a little cover to shoot from should the need arise. In fact, you could always tell the new guys because they'd spend half the night digging vast craters big enough to park a jeep in. Sensible grunts dug little slit trenches just long enough to get your body into and deep enough to get your head down. Anything else was wasted energy, and sensible grunts seldom wasted energy unless they were ordered to do so.

On rare occasions, you had to spend whole nights in your fighting hole because the Viet Cong made it perfectly clear they were not going to let you sleep. Usually, however, they were not so considerate; they'd let you get to sleep first, then wake you up. You always dug your fighting hole right by the entrance to your poncho tent so that, when you were abruptly awakened in the middle of the night, you didn't have to waste time trying to wake up enough to remember where your fighting hole was. I got so good, I could grab my rifle, throw on my flak jacket and helmet, and be lying in my fighting hole without ever opening my eyes or rising more than eight inches off the ground. It took about two-tenths of a second.

Of course, you didn't always sleep in the bushes (we called them the "boonies" or boondocks). During the first eight months I was in Vietnam, from February to September 1967, my battalion was located in the same place continuously, and the battalion headquarters and the four rifle companies each had more or less permanent command posts. You might go on patrol for a few days or even weeks, but somebody always stayed behind, and you always returned to the same place. Since I was in battalion intelligence, when I wasn't in the field, I always worked out of the battalion command post.

Thus, I got to live in relative luxury, for the living shelters at battalion CP were strongback tents. (We called them hooches. Any living quarters more permanent than a simple tent were called hooches, including the houses of the Vietnamese.) Strongback tents were not really tents at all, but rather plywood one-room houses with canvas roofs built by the Sea Bees. They had plywood frames and plywood floors, a walk-in screen door at either end, and screen-covered windows with hinged plywood covers that could be raised out to form plywood awnings. The whole structure was draped with a large general purpose tent that formed the roof.

Strongbacks were very roomy, sleeping eight to twelve men on fold-up cots, and when the camp generator was working, you got electric light from naked bulbs suspended from the roof beams— though, of course, there was no running water or plumbing. If you were lucky, you had an air mattress as well (which we called "rubber ladies" — not nearly so good as the real thing, but quite comfortable under the circumstances), and you could use empty wooden artillery shell boxes as storage compartments and foot lockers. Some guys even had mosquito nets. I had a mosquito net on my cot for awhile, but I got rid of it after the night the battalion CP got hit by a VC rocket attack.

This was not your ordinary everyday artillery or mortar assault. These were real rockets: Russian-made self-propelled 130 millimeter rockets which were aimed by pointing them in the general direction of the target and launched from bamboo chutes. They had been used previously against the big airbase at Danang, but I believe we were the first field unit in the Vietnam war to be introduced to the Russian rockets. History in the making.

There was always noise at night in Vietnam: aircraft, helicopters, artillery, small-arms fire, you name it. If you were to jump at everything, you would never get any sleep ever. So without really trying, you learned quickly to identify sounds in your sleep. The big guns in the CP — we had three different artillery batteries and an 81 millimeter mortar platoon — could fire all night, and though they shook your hooch and nearly blew out your eardrums, you never woke up. But the slightest sound out of the ordinary and your brain would shout, "Wake up; I think there's trouble," and you'd be up and running for the nearest of the deep sandbagged open bunkers that surrounded the hooches before you even knew what was happening.

So while none of us had ever heard rockets before, and though everybody in my hooch was sound asleep at the time, the instant that strange whooshing sound broke the regular nonsilence of the Vietnam night, there was a mad scramble of bodies piling out the door and diving headlong into the nearest bunker, ending up in a cursing, laughing, confused tangle of arms, legs, elbows, wrenched knees, bent backs, jammed fingers and bloody noses many seconds before the first rockets impacted. (Time plays funny tricks in stress situations, as anyone who's ever been in an automobile accident knows. Things which take only a few seconds seem to unravel in slow motion, leaving vivid recollections of each small detail etched into the memory.)

You could see the rockets coming in two waves, the first wave already at the apex of their trajectory, the second still rising out of the horizon to the south. They were relatively slow-moving, and made a very loud noise like water rushing from a high-pressure fire hose; and each rocket left a thin orange trail of sparks and fire like an aerial torpedo. It was curious and novel, and we all watched for awhile (maybe a second or two), until we realized the rockets were right on target and had to paste ourselves to the bottom of the open bunker as the earth around us erupted in columns of smoke, noise, sand, shattered wood, shredded canvas, steel slivers and fire.

Our hooch was not hit, and nobody in my bunker got wounded. But in the rush to get out of the hooch, I had gotten wrapped up in my mosquito net, tripped over another cot, and hit the door frame with my shoulder on the way out the door. It didn't slow me down at all, but it hurt like hell and I ended up with a bruised shin and a very sore shoulder. The morning after the rocket attack, I traded my mosquito net to a guy from Baltimore for a fine pair of padded cartridge belt suspenders he'd swiped off a soldier at the U.S. Army compound in Hoi An the week before. He was happy with the deal, and so was I. I didn't tell him about my shin or my shoulder. And I never used a mosquito net again. Damn things didn't work all that well anyway; every time you got under the net, a whole bunch of the little bastards would climb in with you, and you'd have to spend the rest of the night trying to squash them all.

I thought the good life was over forever when the battalion had to leave its old digs south of Danang and head up north toward the Demilitarized Zone. From then on, we spent a whole lot of time living in one-man poncho tents while we humped through the boondocks in search of the wily VC and their "big brothers," the North Vietnamese regular army. No more strongback hooches, or electricity or weekly cold showers. No more greasy field kitchens with their three tubs of scalding water — one with soap and a toilet brush to swab out your mess kit, two to rinse and sterilize it. No more comfortable walk-up four-hole sit-down outhouses. From here on, it was going to be candles and Coleman gas lanterns, wash when and where you can, eat out of cans, and dig a little cat hole to shit in.

But we did sit still occasionally for a few weeks at a time, and then we'd dig right in like busy beavers and fix up a home. The first place we sat in, after two weeks in the field on Operation Medina in early October 1967, was a new airfield the Sea Bees were building near Ai Tu, between Quang Tri and Dong Ha. We provided security for the Sea Bees, and the intelligence scouts had a little section of the perimeter overlooking a river. The river was right there, not twenty feet away; the current was swift and the water was clean, and you could swim and bathe at the same time, a few guys in the water while others posted guard on the bank. It was really very pleasant.

Anyway, the first night there, I just threw up a one-man poncho tent, dug a fighting hole in the sandy soil, and went to sleep. I was tired. Unfortunately, the wily VC were not. Middle of the night, here comes the welcoming committee: you could hear them dropping in before the first mortar rounds exploded — 20 or 30 of them before the VC let up. We took a whole lot of casualties that night, and though none of the scouts were hit, me and Kenny Takenaga and Rolly Maas decided the next morning that what we needed were real fortifications. No more of this getting up in the middle of the night crap.

We spent the whole day building a magnificent three-man hooch. First we dug a rectangular pit large enough to sleep three and about eighteen inches deep. Then we filled a mess of sandbags (I filled a lot of sandbags in thirteen months; I never go to the beach anymore without having to deliberately force myself not to try to calculate how many sandbags it would take to make the beach completely disappear), lined the pit with them, and added three more layers above ground, making a total inside vertical wall of about three feet. To the head and foot walls we added two more rows of sandbags, each shorter than the one below, to form a sloped roof support so that rain water would be carried off. Then we bummed a two-by-four board from the Sea Bees to use as a roof beam, and hooked two of our ponchos together over the center beam to form the actual roof. The third poncho we used as a ground cloth. We got a Coleman lantern and hung it from the roof beam, removed a few sandbags from one wall to form an entrance, and by damned if we didn't have the finest house on the block — sleeping quarters, reading room and fighting hole all in one. A regular fortified bedroom. Real estate values soared.

As the fortunes of war would have it, of course, the battalion headed back into the field before we ever got the chance to see how well our castle would hold up under siege, but I sure slept soundly for those few weeks there by the river.

Which is more than I can say for one particularly memorable

night on Operation Kentucky just a week or so later. We had formed a perimeter for the night on a hilltop somewhere between Dong Ha and Con Thien. I had thrown up my trusty poncho tent, and dug my fighting hole—but I had neglected to bother digging the little trench around the base of the tent that helps divert rain water rather than allowing it to flow in under the tent. Some people have to learn everything the hard way—though I must say in my defense that I was used to the sandier soil farther south that absorbed rain water quickly. Anyway, I woke up in the middle of the night to discover that it was pouring down rain and, because I was on a hillside, I was lying in the middle of a small but furious river. I was totally, irredeemably soaked, and very cold, and there wasn't a damned thing I could do about it by then. So I just lay there shivering in the water until dawn. It was the longest night of my life, and I never made that mistake again. About the only good thing I can say for the night is that the vc didn't bother to hassle us—no doubt they were all trying to stay dry.

The next place the battalion went, just before Thanksgiving 1967, was Con Thien, one of the northernmost Marine outposts along the DMZ. No need for one-man poncho tents there; we all lived in damp, muddy underground sandbagged bunkers just like the Doughboys in France. I liked the house by the river much better. But after thirty-three days of "Over There" and "Mademoiselle from Armentiers," we were sent back down to a place just south of Quang Tri where we spent the next month. Me and Randy Hill scrounged up a good-sized tent from an anti-tank battalion big enough to stand up in, threw in two cots swiped from the battalion first aid station (no one can scrounge like a Marine; if you can't scrounge in the Marine Corps, you don't get nothin'), and we were in business.

Of course, since this was the monsoon season, you were wet all the time. The temperature seldom went below 55 or 60 degrees, but because you were always wet and because your body was accustomed to temperatures into the hundreds, it was cold. (I even had a pair of long underwear dyed green and sent over as a Christmas present by my mother. Everything you wore was green. Even the small white V of a teeshirt sticking up below the neck stood out like a bullseye on a clear night.) At night, you slept with your clothes on, which were wet, under a wet blanket. But if you put your poncho over your blanket, the sealed rubber kept the heat in, and after awhile you would warm up from your own body heat. You were still wet when you woke up, because moisture condensed on the inside of the poncho, but you stayed warm and toasty. It wasn't so bad.

In fact, New Year's Eve, when Randy and I sat on ammo boxes in front of the tent watching the fireworks display, we were feeling like princes. We had a pint of Johnny Walker Red Label scotch that John Pifer, a high school buddy, had mailed to me stuffed inside a hollowed out loaf of French bread. (A few years later, I helped Pifer get a Conscientious Objector's deferment from the draft—I owed him one for the scotch, and I couldn't see anybody else having to learn about Vietnam the hard way if he could avoid it.) At midnight, flares of every imaginable color and kind went up— against orders—from every Marine outpost all the way to the DMZ. Happy New Year! It was beautiful. It made us homesick. Everything made us homesick. The next day, Randy and I celebrated the New Year with a picnic thrown together from the ingredients of care packages from home: salami, cheese, saltines, raisins, chocolate and cookies all laid out on top of a box of 81 millimeter mortar rounds. The sun even made a cameo appearance, and it was a grand way to begin another year.

Finally, toward the end of January, the battalion was sent down to the big base at Phu Bai for a rest after four months constantly on the move. We got to live in strongback tents again, and with only a month to go in Vietnam, I thought I was going out in style and comfort. Ah, but the fortunes of war—just a few days later, I found myself in Hue City in the middle of the biggest battle of the war: the Tet Offensive of 1968. I spent the next month mostly not sleeping at all, and when I did sleep, it was wherever I could put my head—in abandoned houses, in abandoned convents, in abandoned churches, in abandoned businesses (everything was abandoned). But at least you didn't have to build anything. Or dig anything. And sometimes you found an old mattress to sleep on. It was better than a shelter half, and no questions asked.

THE UNITED STATES
SCREW & BOLT COMPANY

McGeorge Bundy: Special assistant to presidents Kennedy and Johnson for national security affairs, 1961–66. Described in *The Pentagon Papers* as the "principal architect of U.S. Vietnam policy." Became president of the Ford Foundation.

Michael Pacek: As a child, survived the Nazi occupation of Czechoslovakia and the subsequent Soviet takeover; family later escaped to the U.S. Enlisted in the Marine Corps in 1958; reenlisted in 1961; sent to Vietnam as a "military advisor" in 1963. After two combat missions, had flashbacks of Czechoslovakia and refused to participate in any more fighting. Courtmartialed, he was sentenced to five years in military prison and given a dishonorable discharge.

Roswell L. Gilpatric: Deputy Secretary of Defense, 1961–64. In April 1961, he headed a task force study group that recommended the U.S. impress friends and foes alike that "come what may, the U.S. intends to *win* this battle." Became a director of CBS and Eastern Airlines, and chairman of the board of Fairchild Camera & Instrument Corporation and the Federal Reserve Bank of New York.

Randall Moore: Pennridge High School, Perkasie, Pennsylvania, class of 1965; enlisted in the U.S. Army paratroopers. Killed in Vietnam in 1966 when a companion's grenade accidentally exploded.

U. Alexis Johnson: Deputy Undersecretary of State, 1961–64 and

65–66; Deputy Ambassador to South Vietnam, 1964–65. In October 1961, he estimated that three divisions (about 102,000 men) of American troops would be needed to defeat the Viet Cong. Continued his distinguished career in foreign service, culminating with chief U.S. delegate to the Strategic Arms Limitation Talks.

Maynard Hager: Pennridge High School, Perkasie, Pennsylvania, class of 1964; an honorably discharged Marine sergeant, he served two full tours in Vietnam. He died in a motorcycle accident in Sellersville, Pa., in 1971. (As of 1976, the Indochina Resource Center had recorded 55,000 Vietnam veterans dead of suicide, drug overdose, and single-car or motorcycle accidents.)

Robert S. McNamara: Secretary of Defense, 1961–68. In November 1961, he estimated that the maximum U.S. ground forces required for victory in South Vietnam would not exceed six divisions (about 205,000 men), even in the face of overt Chinese intervention. In a 1964 memo to Lyndon Johnson, he said that "the South Vietnam conflict is regarded as a test case." Became president of the World Bank.

Terry Samuels: Discharged from the Marines as unfit, he got his draft status changed so that he could enlist in the Army. "I was red, white, and blue all the way [but] I went to mental hygiene at Cu Chi about six months after I got [to Vietnam] and told them my head was getting pretty messed up. . . . I only kept track of the innocent people I killed, the civilians, prisoners, a lot of NVA and VC who we'd captured and who I'd been told to 'take care of.' It came to 37." He deserted and made his way to Canada.

Admiral Harry D. Felt: Commander of all U.S. forces in the Pacific, 1958–64. In January 1963, he predicted victory in South Vietnam within three years. Became director of Telecheck International, Inc., and advisor to the board of directors of the Crocker Bank.

John Blass: With an IQ of 49 and a sixth grade education, Blass would clearly have been disqualified from the draft had he reported for his pre-induction physical. He did not. It is doubtful that he even understood what his draft notice meant. He was convicted of draft evasion and sentenced to federal prison.

Dean Rusk: Secretary of State, 1961–69. In August 1963, he argued that U.S. policy be based on the premise that "we will not pull out of Vietnam until the war is won." Appointed Silbey Professor of International Law at the University of Georgia.

Ron Kovic: Enlisted in the U.S. Marine Corps in 1964; wounded in action in Vietnam, he was permanently paralyzed from the waist down. "My penis will never get hard again. I didn't even have time to learn how to enjoy it and now it is gone, it is dead, it is as numb as the rest of me." (One of 21,000 permanently disabled Vietnam veterans.)

Henry Cabot Lodge: Ambassador to South Vietnam, 1963–64, 65–67. In August 1963, he told John Kennedy that U.S. prestige was publicly committed in Vietnam and that "there is no turning back." In June 1964, he predicted that bombing North Vietnam would cause Viet Cong support in the South to fade away. Became in succession Ambassador-at-Large, Ambassador to Germany, chief negotiator at the Paris Peace Talks, and Ambassador to the Vatican.

James Wilson: Convicted in 1966 of violating the August 1965 amendment to the Selective Service Law, which made it a crime to knowingly destroy or mutilate a draft card; sentenced to three years in federal prison. (Congressman Mendel Rivers described the purpose of the amendment as "a straightforward clear answer to those who would make a mockery of our efforts in South Vietnam. . . . This is the least we can do for our men in South Vietnam fighting to preserve freedom.")

General Paul D. Harkins: Commander of all U.S. forces in South Vietnam, 1962–64. Cabled Maxwell Taylor in October 1963: "On balance we are gaining in contest with the VC. There will continue to be minor ups and downs but the general trend continues upward." Became advisor to the American Security Council in Boston.

Kenneth G. Worman: Pennridge High School, Perkasie, Pennsylvania, class of 1966; enlisted in the U.S. Army. From a letter to the author's parents, datelined Duc Pho, 3 May 67: "I've been here since February and it seems like two years. I just hope the rest of my time does not go so slow. I received the candy you sent the other day and would like to thank you very much at this time and so would the rest of the platoon. For when you receive a package out here it belongs to everyone. How is Billy doing? [The author, in Vietnam also at that time.] Just fine, I hope. Would you please send me his address so I could write." Killed in action later that month.

Cyrus R. Vance: Secretary of the Army, 1962–63; Deputy Secretary of Defense, 1964–67; chief negotiator to the Paris Peace Talks, 1968–69. In 1964, along with McGeorge Bundy and Llewellyn Thompson, became responsible for approving in advance South Vietnamese covert operations against North Vietnam including ambush, sapper and kidnapping teams, and aerial and naval bombardment. Appointed Secretary of State by Jimmy Carter in 1977.

John Spencer: Formerly PFC, 3rd Battalion, 7th Marine Regiment, Vietnam 1966–67, Purple Heart Medal. Treated with morphine for wounds received in combat, he discovered that the morphine began "relieving my tension about going back into combat. Then I got to using heroin and that was it." After returning to the U.S. and receiving his discharge, he "went to the VA looking for help. There was none. So I went to robbery and stealing to support my habit. Then I got busted." (During the late sixties and well into the seventies, the U.S. prison population included a disproportionate number of Vietnam veterans. A June 1973 report by the Federal Bureau of Prisons stated that 32 percent of the country's federal prisoners were veterans. Through the sixties and well into the seventies, the Veterans Administration refused to acknowledge drug addiction as a Vietnam-related problem.)

William P. Bundy: Assistant, then Deputy Secretary of Defense for International Security Affairs, 1961–64; Assistant Secretary of State for East Asian and Pacific Affairs, 1964–69. One of the chief planners of Johnson's full-scale bombing campaign of North Vietnam, in a June 1964 memo he argued for a Congressional resolution as a "continuing demonstration of U.S. firmness and for complete flexibility in the hands of the Executive." This was fully two months before the Tonkin Gulf incident. Became a senior research associate at the Massachusetts Institute of Technology's Center for International Studies, then editor of the prestigious *Foreign Affairs* magazine.

David Taube: Enlisting in the U.S. Army Reserve in 1966, he was called up for active duty in March 1967. "I concluded that if I were to kill innocent Vietnamese, I could not live with myself. Canada seemed nicer than jail." (Of the 50,000 political fugitives during the Vietnam war, most fled to other countries — the largest U.S. exodus since the Revolutionary War.)

John A. McCone: Director of the Central Intelligence Agency, 1961–65. Sided with McNamara and Rusk in arguing for a Congressional resolution allowing the Executive a freer hand in the Vietnam war. The argument pre-dated the Gulf of Tonkin incident by several months. McCone became the chairman of Hendy International Corporation, director of International Telephone & Telegraph, and director of Standard Oil of California.

Willie Jordan: A Mississippi civil rights worker, he reported for induction into the army "a few minutes late, and induction station officials refused to process him." Convicted of draft evasion, he was sentenced to five years in federal prison.

Representative Thomas E. Morgan: Chairman of the House Foreign Affairs Committee, he sponsored the Gulf of Tonkin Resolution through the House. Subsequently re-elected to six more terms in the House.

Timothy Clover: Receiving his draft notice in 1967, he was inducted into the army. Upon receiving orders to Vietnam, his father writes, "he had to decide which way he would give up his freedom. He could refuse to go to Vietnam and face jail and a dishonorable discharge; he could leave the United States and become an exile from his family and the country he loved; or he could participate in a war which he was convinced was completely immoral. For the sake of his young wife and baby boy, Tim chose to accept Vietnam. He made this choice so that their son would have no stigma to bear, such as our society places on its citizens who refuse to fight wars and kill other human beings." Clover was killed in action in May 1968.

J. William Fulbright: Chairman of the Senate Foreign Relations Committee, he sponsored the Gulf of Tonkin Resolution through the Senate. He was subsequently re-elected, serving until 1975.

John O. Sumrall: Black civil rights worker from Mississippi. "If I am not looked upon as an equal citizen in everyday life, why am I looked upon as an equal citizen when it comes time for me to report for induction? I'm going to stay here and fight the *real* battle for freedom." Convicted of draft evasion in 1968, he was sentenced to five years in federal prison and fined $2500.

William H. Sullivan: Held various high posts in the State Department under Kennedy and Johnson including Ambassador to Laos and chairman of the interagency Vietnam coordinating committee. In December 1964, he persuaded Laotian Premier Souvanna Phouma to permit U.S. airstrikes against NVA infiltration routes in southern Laos. Went on to serve as Deputy Assistant Secretary of State for East Asian and Pacific Affairs, Ambassador to the Philippines, and Ambassador to Iran.

Tom Kenny: Formerly sergeant, 26th Infantry Division, Vietnam; medically discharged with undiagnosed symptoms, he was awarded $146 per month for a skin rash. The undiagnosed symptoms include vomitting blood, temporary paralysis, perpetual skin rash, numbness, blackouts, and loss of sexual drive—the same symptoms as those of dioxin poisoning caused by exposure to the chemical defoliant Agent Orange. The VA has concluded that Kenny's records indicate no exposure to Agent Orange, and as of September 1979 has refused Kenny treatment. He is visibly dying.

General Maxwell D. Taylor: Chairman of the Joint Chiefs of Staff, 1962–64; Ambassador to South Vietnam, 1964–65; special consultant to the president, 1965–69. As ambassador in December 1964, speaking to a group of South Vietnamese army generals including Nguyen Cao Ky, Nguyen Van Thieu, and Nguyen Khanh (all of whom were past or future heads of government), Taylor began: "Do you all understand English?" He became chairman of the Foreign Intelligence Advisory Board and member of the board of the Institute for Defense Analysis.

Gary Samuels: Drafted into the army in 1969 after graduating from Bloomfield College, he was assigned to the 198th Light Infantry Brigade in Vietnam. Wounded in a misdirected barrage of U.S. artillery, his left leg was amputated below the knee. (One of 5,000 amputees among U.S. servicemen in Vietnam.)

Admiral Ulysses S. Grant Sharp, Jr.: Commander of all U.S. forces in the Pacific, 1964–68. In January 1966, he cabled the Joint Chiefs that bombing North Vietnam's oil supplies would "bring the enemy to the conference table or cause the insurgency to wither from lack of support." Became consultant to the president of Teledyne Ryan Aerospace Corporation.

Jim Fallows: A Harvard senior in 1969, he dieted until his weight dropped below the minimum required for induction and received an exemption from the draft. "I was overcome by a wave of relief, which for the first time revealed to me how great my terror had been, and by the beginning of the sense of shame that remains with me to this day."

Walt W. Rostow: Senior White House specialist on Southeast Asia, holding various titles between 1961–69. In a December 1966 memo, he found the American/South Vietnamese position "greatly improved" and predicted dominance and possibly victory by the end of 1967. Appointed professor of economics and history at the University of Texas.

Robert Muller: Formerly 1st Lt., 2nd Battalion, 3rd Marine Regiment, Vietnam 1968–69. Wounded in action; permanently paralyzed from the fifth thoracic vertebra down. "Don't use me as a rallying cry to continue this war for a just peace, to throw more guys and more of my friends and brothers into the hopper of this war machine. . . . If I can recognize my loss is a waste, why can't you?"

John C. Stennis: As chairman of the Senate Preparedness Subcommittee, he declared in January 1967 that Westmoreland's troop requests should be met "even if it should require mobilization or partial mobilization" of the entire country. Became chairman of the Armed Services Committee of the Senate.

Sandy Scheuer: A junior majoring in speech therapy at the Speech and Hearing Clinic of Kent State University, she often did volunteer work with poor people who had speech defects. One of four students killed in action by the Ohio National Guard in May 1970.

Robert W. Komer: Special assistant to the president under various titles, 1961–67; deputy to the commander of U.S. forces in Vietnam, 1967–68. In a February 1967 report to Lyndon Johnson, Komer stated: "Wastefully, expensively, but indisputably, we are winning the war in the South." In succession, appointed Ambassador to Turkey, senior social science researcher for the Rand Corporation, and advisor to the Secretary of Defense for NATO Affairs.

Dean Kahler: One of nine Kent State University students wounded in action by the Ohio National Guard in May 1970, he is permanently paralyzed from the waist down and remains confined to a wheelchair.

General William C. Westmoreland: Commander of all U.S. forces in Vietnam, 1964–68. Lyndon Johnson: "When we add divisions, can't the enemy add divisions? If so, where does it all end?" Westmoreland: "That is a good question." Decorated for meritorious service in Vietnam, and promoted to Army Chief of Staff.

Phillip L. Gibbs: Husband, father, and pre-law student at Jackson State College, Mississippi. Killed in action by Jackson police and Mississippi highway patrolmen in May 1970. One of two dead, the other, James Green, a 17-year-old high school student returning home from his parttime job near the Jackson State campus.

General Earle G. Wheeler: Chairman of the Joint Chiefs of Staff, 1964–70. Cabled Westmoreland in February 1968: "United States is not prepared to accept defeat in Vietnam. If you need more troops, ask for them." Retired to his 180-acre farm in West Virginia.

John Beitzel: Formerly sergeant, Americal Division, Vietnam 1969–70. "I looked around for a job after I came back, but I couldn't find any. And here I'd gone over and fought so that I could live in this country, and I couldn't even get a job. You know, they say, 'Well, you aren't trained in anything'; and the only thing I had been trained in was to kill. I had been trained in the infantry, and there wasn't a market for that over here. So I couldn't get a job. Before I went over, they said, 'You're 1-A and you'll probably get drafted, so you can't get a job.' So I went over and got rid of the 1-A, did the military duty and then I came back, and they still wouldn't hire me."

Clark Clifford: Secretary of Defense, 1968–69. Headed the "Clifford Group," a high-ranking study group convened at the request of Lyndon Johnson in February 1968 to review U.S. policy in Vietnam. Recommended that the American "presence in South Vietnam should be used 'to buy time' during which the South

Vietnamese Army and Government can develop effective capability." States *The Pentagon Papers*: "Faced with a fork in the road of our Vietnam policy, the working group failed to seize the opportunity to change directions. Indeed they seemed to recommend that we continue rather haltingly down the same road." Became a senior partner of Clifford, Warnke, Glass, McIlwain & Finney, and a director of Phillips Petroleum and the Knight-Ridder newspaper chain.

Larry Rottmann: Formerly 1st Lt., 25th Infantry Division, Vietnam 1967–68, Bronze Star. At Christmas 1967, Rottmann sent a Christmas card to various members of Congress containing a photograph depicting a white medic, a black medic, and a Vietnamese treating another wounded Vietnamese. The photo was captioned with a quote from General William T. Sherman: "I am sick and tired of war. Its glory is all moonshine. It is only those who have never fired a shot nor heard the shrieks and groans of the wounded who cry aloud for blood, more vengeance, more desolation and destruction. War is cruel and you cannot refine it. War is hell." Upon release from active duty, Rottmann became a vocal member of Vietnam Veterans Against the War. In 1970, courtmartial proceedings were instituted against him, charging him with printing and distributing the 1967 card at government expense. Only after a determined challenge by the American Civil Liberties Union were the charges dropped.

Richard Helms: Deputy Director, then Director of the Central Intelligence Agency, 1965–73. Member of the "Clifford Group." Appointed Ambassador to Iran.

Scott Camil: Formerly sergeant, 1st Battalion, 4th Marine Regiment, Vietnam 1966–67. In 1971, Camil said to U.S. Senator Gurney of Florida: "Senator Gurney, the Vietnamese government doesn't represent the Vietnamese people." Gurney's reply: "So what? The American government doesn't represent the American people." The following year, Camil was indicted as a member of the so-called "Gainesville VVAW Conspiracy."

Nicholas deB. Katzenbach: Deputy, then Acting, then Attorney General, 1962–66; Undersecretary of State, 1966–69. Member of the "Clifford Group." Became vice president, general counsel and director of the IBM Corporation.

Ron Ferrizzi: Vietnam veteran who joined a group from VVAW that went to Washington, DC, in April 1971, to return their war decorations to Congress. "My parents told me that if I really did come down here and turned in my medals, that they never wanted anything to do with me. My wife said she would divorce me if I came down here because she wanted my medals for our son to see when he grows up. I'm not proud of these medals. I'm not proud of what I did to receive them."

Paul C. Warnke: General Counsel, then Assistant Secretary of Defense, 1966–69. Member of the "Clifford Group." Returned to private law practice with Clifford, Warnke, Glass, McIlwain & Finney; in 1977 replaced U. Alexis Johnson as chief SALT negotiator.

Peter P. Mahoney: Formerly 1st Lt., U.S. Army, Vietnam 1970–71, Bronze Star, Cross of Gallantry. One of seven honorably discharged members of Vietnam Veterans Against the War indicted in the "Gainesville VVAW Conspiracy," Mahoney was charged in August 1972 with allegedly conspiring to cause riots during the Republican National Convention with fire-bombs, automatic weapons, and slingshot-propelled explosives. The penalty for conviction: five years and $10,000. More than a year later, after only three-and-a-half hours of deliberation, the trial jury found all of the defendants not guilty. Said one juror: "[The government] had nothing on those boys." (Heading the investigation of the Gainesville conspiracy was Guy L. Goodwin, chief of the Special Litigation Division of the Internal Security Division of the U.S. Justice Department. Goodwin had just previously headed the investigation of the "Harrisburg Seven"—Father Daniel Berrigan and six other defendants charged with conspiring to kidnap Henry Kissinger. That trial also resulted in acquittal of all the defendants.)

Paul H. Nitze: Assistant Secretary of Defense, 1961–63; Secretary of the Navy, 1963–67; Deputy Secretary of Defense, 1967–69. Member of the "Clifford Group." Became chairman of the board of Aspen Skiing Corporation, and director of Schroder's Inc., American Security & Trust Co., Atlantic Council, and Potomac Associates.

Eugene A. Reyes: Formerly USMC, Vietnam 1969–70. After completing his full tour of duty in Vietnam, Reyes returned to the U.S. and deserted in August 1971. Arrested by the FBI in March 1974, he was courtmartialed, given a Bad Conduct Discharge, and sent to prison. ("One-fifth of all deserters never actually evaded Vietnam service. They finished full combat tours before running afoul of military discipline back home, often because of post-combat readjustment problems." About 250,000 Vietnam-era veterans received Undesirable, Bad Conduct, or Dishonorable Discharges, each of which automatically bars the recipient from all Veterans Administration benefits. Only 13 percent of these discharges were awarded by the judicial process of courtmartial; the rest were issued through various administrative proceedings.)

Philip C. Habib: Deputy Assistant Secretary of State for East Asian and Pacific Affairs under William Bundy. Member of the "Clifford Group." Went on to continue a distinguished career in the foreign service.

Andrew Gettler: Vietnam veteran honorably discharged from the army in 1968. Began seeking employment assistance from the VA in 1974: "The treatment I received at the VA was brusque, impolite, and conveyed a sort of 'What do you expect for nothing' attitude. I was not looking for a handout, merely assistance of a practical nature, i.e. job listings, vocational training, etc., but I couldn't even get a civil response to my inquiries. At the [New York City] Mayor's Office of Veterans Affairs, the story was just as dismal." Finally in 1975, still unable to find work, he applied for welfare through the one office of the New York City Human Resources Administration designated to handle all Vietnam veterans and their families: "90 percent of the caseworkers are women over 40 whose major contact with the war was the six o'clock news. They are, as a group, the rudest, most callous, most off-hand people it has ever been my misfortune to deal with. I have been involved with these people for over a year now, and every day has been a struggle. I have had to fight every step of the way." (In 1976, the Indochina Resource Center stated that the rate of unemployment among Vietnam veterans was substantially higher than that of their peers, Vietnam veterans constituting one of the largest single groups of unemployed in the nation.)

Harold Brown: Secretary of the Air Force, 1965–69. In March 1968, he advocated intensified bombing of North Vietnam without "concern for collateral civilian damage and casualties" in an effort to "erode the will of the population by exposing a wider area of North Vietnam to casualties and destruction." In 1977, Jimmy Carter appointed Brown Secretary of Defense.

Lewis H. Hitchcock: Honorably discharged Indochina veteran. During his active duty separation physical examination, a Specialist 5 (equivalent to a sergeant) determined that Hitchcock's hearing was equal to that of a 98-year-old. He applied for disability compensation, and was retested by an army doctor of officer rank who found his hearing to be "the maximum loss one can incur without being considered disabled." Reapplying to the VA for compensation, he was referred by the VA to a civilian audiologist who confirmed the original tests. The VA then determined Hitchcock's disability to be service-connected but less than 10 percent, and thus not compensable. "The hearing of a 98-year-old and unable to hear in the classroom and not compensable! Not even worth a measly $32 per month. . . . I used to be patriotic."

Creighton W. Abrams: Commanding General of all U.S. forces in Vietnam, 1968–72. Presiding over the U.S. plan to "buy time" while the South Vietnamese army and government developed "effective capability," Abrams was in charge of "Vietnamizing" the Vietnam war. He was promoted to Army Chief of Staff.

Geoffrey Childs: "If it is important, I was once-upon-a-time the commanding officer of A Company, 1/35th Infantry, 4th Infantry Division. I used to think that was in another life, but in a strange way I suppose it is probably more a part of my present than it has ever been. I have a theory that once you have violated the most sacred law and taken another life, the structure that permitted it, that encouraged it, rings kind of hollow ever after. Nowadays I make a living climbing and writing about it. It's not much of a living, actually, but it's better than a lot of things."

Ellsworth Bunker: Ambassador to South Vietnam, 1967–73. In 1970, he received the American Statesman Award from the Freedom Foundation. He was subsequently appointed Ambassador-at-Large.

Nick Patrick: Formerly USMC, two tours in Vietnam, three Purple Hearts, Silver Star, Bronze Star. New Jersey state Veterans of Foreign Wars Commander Thomas Blesedell: "We're concerned that Vietnam veterans are not joining [VFW], are not having concern for the flag. It makes me proud to see the colors out." Patrick's response: "My leg is put together with chewing gum and wire and he's gonna tell me I don't care about the flag? That's why no Vietnam vets are joining."

Spiro T. Agnew: Vice President of the United States, 1969–73. Of the antiwar movement, Agnew said: "Malcontents, radicals, incendiaries, civil and uncivil disobedients, yippies, hippies, yahoos, Black Panthers, lions and tigers—I would swap the whole damn zoo for a single platoon of the kind of young Americans I saw in Vietnam." He was permitted to resign from office and plead *nolo contendere* to charges of official corruption; he served no time in prison, and was publicly wined and dined by such people as Frank Sinatra.

Hans Ebner, Jr.: Formerly U.S. Army, Vietnam 1964–65. "I can't seem to purge myself of the rage. You'd think after all these years that I'd have my thoughts straightened out, but it's no better now. I probably should be in a VA hospital or something, but my wounds don't show." (In October 1979, the VA began Operation Outreach, a three-year program to address Vietnam veterans' readjustment problems: four-and-a-half years after the collapse of South Vietnam, six-and-a-half years after U.S. troops were officially withdrawn from Vietnam, fourteen-and-a-half years after the first U.S. combat units entered Vietnam, eighteen years after the first U.S. military advisors entered Vietnam. As late as 1976, the VA did not acknowledge the existence of so-called Post-Vietnam Syndrome [Post Traumatic Stress Disorder].

Richard M. Nixon: President of the United States, 1969–74. Of amnesty for Vietnam-era draft resisters, exiles, deserters and veterans with less-than-honorable discharges, Nixon said it was "the most immoral thing I can think of.... I can think of no greater insult to the memories of those who fought and died, to those who have served, and also to our POWs, to say to them that we are now going to provide amnesty for those who deserted the country." He was permitted to resign from office rather than face impeachment charges, and was subsequently given a full pardon by Gerald Ford, a pension, and an expense account.

John Glenn: Formerly a Navy Medical Corpsman attached to the Marine Corps in Vietnam. His brother Andrew wrote: "He shot himself last year, seven years after his discharge. Vietnam Syndrome? I saw it coming. . . . My brother's heart no longer soars like the hawk/ nor his talons skim the dark earth/ He turned his talons on himself/ Show me the way down to the dark chamber/ where I might find him clutching the flower of forgiveness/ that I might unfold his fist. . . ." (As of 1976, according to the Indochina Resource Center, half a million Vietnam veterans have attempted suicide since returning home.)

Henry A. Kissinger: Director of the National Security Council, 1969–75; Secretary of State, 1973–77. October 1972: "Peace is at hand." Became a professor at Georgetown University, consultant to NBC and Goldman Sachs & Company, and a bestselling author.

Robert L. Schlosser: Formerly U.S. Army, Indochina veteran, 1969–70. He spent his time in Thailand "surrounded by U.S. Air Force bases that sent bombers over Laos, Cambodia and Vietnam every day of every one of those fourteen months I spent guarding bombs and picking up stoned and drunk soldiers out of alleys. So what do we have now? Winnebagos. McDonald's hamburgers. Was Vietnam real? Is television real? Or the state of contemporary America? Ah, hell, it don't mean nothing, man."

SOURCE NOTES

Information on government officials comes from *The Pentagon Papers* (PP), Sheehan, Smith, Kenworthy, Butterfield, and the *New York Times* staff; Bantam Books, 1971; and from various editions of *Who's Who in America.*
McG. Bundy: PP, p. 630.
Pacek: *Chance & Circumstance* (C&C), Lawrence M. Baskir & William A. Strauss; Vintage Books, 1978, p. 140.
Gilpatric: PP, p. 88.
Moore: friend of the author.
U. Johnson: PP, p. 97.
Hager: friend of the author. Statistics from *A Time to Heal* (IRC), Indochina Resource Center Publications, 1976.
McNamara: PP, pp. 85 & 278.
T. Samuels: C&C, p. 111.
Felt: PP, p. 164.
Blass: C&C, p. 98.
Rusk: PP, p. 174.
Kovic: *Born on the Fourth of July*, Ron Kovic, 1976, p. 111. Statistics on disabled veterans from C&C, p. 4.

Lodge: PP, pp. 160 & 250.
Wilson: *We Won't Go* (WWG), Alice Lynd, ed.; Beacon Press, 1968, p. 33.
Harkins: PP, p. 222.
Worman: friend of the author.
Vance: PP, p. 316.
Spencer: *The New Soldier* (TNS), David Thorne & George Butler, eds., Collier Books, 1971, p. 148. Prison statistics from IRC. Information on drugs and the VA from the Morris County *Daily Record*, New Jersey (DR), December 12, 1979.
W. Bundy: PP, p. 257.
Taube: WWG; political fugitive statistics from C&C, p. 167.
McCone: PP, p. 251.
Jordan: C&C, p. 99.
Morgan: PP, p. 264.
Clover: Introduction to *The Leaves of My Trees, Still Green*, poems of Timothy Clover, posthumously published and copyrighted by his father, Lionel Clover, Adams Press, 1970.
Fulbright: PP, p. 264.
Sumrall: WWG, p. 89.
Sullivan: PP, p. 335.
Kenny: *New Jersey* magazine (NJ), September 1979.
Taylor: PP, p. 337.
G. Samuels: NJ; amputee figure from C&C, p. 4.
Sharp: PP, p. 476.
Fallows: C&C, p. 254.
Rostow: PP, p. 525.
Muller: TNS, p. 104.
Stennis: PP, p. 525.
Scheuer: *Kent State*, James Michener; Random House, 1971.
Komer: PP, p. 555.
Kahler: *New York Times* Index of Abstracts.
Westmoreland: PP, p. 515.
Gibbs: *Newsweek*, May 25, 1970.
Wheeler: PP, p. 594.
Beitzel: testimony before VVAW Philadelphia Winter Soldier Investigation, 1971.
Clifford: PP, pp. 601–2, 604.
Rottmann: TNS, p. 72.
Helms: PP, p. 601.
Camil: TNS, p. 88.
Katzenbach: PP, p. 601.
Ferrizzi: TNS, p. 142.
Warnke: PP, p. 601.
Mahoney: The *New York Times*, September 1, 1973.
Nitze: PP, p. 601.
Reyes: letter to East River Anthology (ERA). Bad discharge statistics from C&C, p. 13.
Habib: PP, p. 601.

Gettler: 2/5/76 letter to ERA.
Brown: PP, p. 606.
Hitchcock: 4/76 letter to ERA.
Abrams: paraphrasing of Clifford quote from PP, p. 602.
Childs: *Demilitarized Zones*, Jan Barry & W. D. Ehrhart, eds., East River Anthology, 1976, p. 98.
Patrick: DR, July 8, 1979.
Agnew: C&C, p. 209.
Ebner: 1976 letter to ERA. VA/PVS information from IRC and DR, December 30, 1979.
Nixon: C&C, p. 208.
Glenn: 1979 letter to the author. Poetry excerpts from "Suicide on Hallow's Eve," unpublished poem by Andrew Glenn.
Schlosser: 1975 letter to ERA.

LEARNING THE HARD WAY

Why should military conscription be of any concern to you? The United States is not at war. There is no active draft taking place at this time, and our national leaders have repeatedly insisted that they are not contemplating a military draft. The current required registration, according to the government, is only a contingency plan to cover the possibility of some unforeseeable national emergency which everyone hopes will never occur. Moreover, half of you — as women — wouldn't even be subject to such an emergency draft under present law. The other half need only register at your local post office when you turn 18, and go about your lives as always until you are too old to be drafted.

But what are the odds that you will reach that magic age which puts you beyond conscription? Fifty percent? Three to two? Five to one? I would not hazard a guess. Consider our government's open hostility toward the Sandinista government of Nicaragua. Consider our massive dependence on Middle Eastern oil, and how our government might respond if that supply is threatened or cut off. Consider that our government is sending millions of dollars of military hardware to support a right-wing government in El Salvador, and that U.S. military personnel are at this moment deployed in that country. Consider that U.S. government policymakers now openly discuss what was utterly unthinkable only a decade ago: the notion that a nuclear war can be winnable.

Consider that in 1980, then–Republican candidate for president

Originally given as a speech to the students of George School, Newtown, Pennsylvania, January 18, 1982.

46

Ronald Reagan criticized President Jimmy Carter's reinstitution of draft registration as needless and inflammatory to world peace, promising that if elected, he would end registration. Soon after his election, however, Mr. Reagan publicly endorsed retention of draft registration.

Finally, consider this: in 1954, then–Senator Lyndon Johnson publicly stated, "I am against sending American GIs into the mud and muck of Indochina on a blood-letting spree to perpetuate colonialism and white man's exploitation of Asia." In 1964, then–President Johnson campaigned successfully for re-election against Barry Goldwater on a promise to keep American GIs out of Vietnam. Four years later, while Lyndon Johnson was still president, nearly half a million American GIs were fighting in the mud and muck of Indochina, and the blood-letting spree would eventually claim the lives of 1.7 million Vietnamese, wounding 3.2 million more, and leaving 12 million homeless.

One of those half million American GIs was me. I was not even drafted; I volunteered. I based my decision on every responsible source of information I had available to me at that time. According to the information I had — information disseminated by my government and all the major news media — Communists from North Vietnam, supported by the Russians and the Chinese, were waging a terrible war of aggression against the free Republic of South Vietnam. Moreover, not only was the freedom of the South Vietnamese at stake, but because Vietnam was part and parcel of the Communist conspiracy ultimately to take over the world, my country's freedom and my own freedom were at stake. It was something called the Domino Theory.

This was all taking place about the time I was your age, and I believed sincerely that if we did not stop the communists in Vietnam, we would one day have to fight them in San Diego. I had no reason up to that point in my life to doubt either my government or my high school teachers or the *New York Times*. I believed in my country and its God-given role as leader of the Free World — that it was the finest nation on earth, that its political system and its leaders were essentially good, and that any nation or people who opposed us must be inherently bad. Furthermore, I valued my freedom, and I took seriously the notion that I owed something to my country. The draft was already cranking into high gear in the spring of 1966 when I decided to turn down four college acceptances and enlist in the United States Marine Corps. I was 17 years old, nine days out of high school.

Seven months later, I found myself in Vietnam. What I found in Vietnam, however, was not at all what I had been taught to expect. The American people had been told that we were defending a free democracy. What I found was a military dictatorship rife with corruption and venality and repression. The premier of South Vietnam openly admired Adolf Hitler. Buddhist priests who petitioned for peace were jailed or shot down in the streets. Officials at every level engaged in blatant black-marketeering at astronomical profit and at the expense of their own people. And the government was clearly devoid of the support of the vast majority of the Vietnamese people.

The American people had been told that some Vietnamese civilians had been mercifully relocated into safe hamlets to protect them from the marauding Viet Cong. What I found was the wholesale forced removal of thousands of people from their ancestral homelands to poverty-stricken, misery-laden shantytowns where men had no work and women rooted through American garbage trying to find food for their children.

The American people had been told that the Viet Cong managed to perpetuate their guerrilla war only through violence and coercion inflicted upon the Vietnamese people: kidnapping, murder, impressment and theft were the tactics of the communists; unspeakable atrocities were visited upon those who refused to cooperate. But in my thirteen months in a Marine infantry battalion, I regularly witnessed and participated in the destruction of civilian homes and sometimes whole villages, the most brutal interrogations of civilians, and the routine killing of unarmed men, women and children along with their crops and livestock.

The American people had been told that we were in Vietnam to defend the Vietnamese against outside aggression, but I found that we were the aggressors, we were the foreigners, and the people we were supposedly defending hated us because we destroyed their forests with chemical defoliants, and burned their fields with napalm, and called the people of Vietnam gooks, chinks, slopes and zipperheads, turning their sons into shoeshine boys and their daughters into whores.

Make no mistake about it: there were indeed Viet Cong in Vietnam. And they regularly tried to kill me. But they had good reason to do so, and most of the people of Vietnam, as nearly as I could tell then and still believe to this day, were on the side of the Viet Cong, wanting little else than for us to stop killing them and go away. In short, I discovered that the information upon which I had based my decision to enlist had been bad information.

For my little part in the war, the government promoted me to sergeant, awarded me the Purple Heart Medal, two Presidential Unit citations, the Navy Combat Action ribbon and the Good Conduct Medal, and gave me an honorable discharge. But I could not avoid the increasingly uncomfortable feeling that my government had been playing the game with less than a full deck of cards, and that I had been had, plain and simple.

Consider this: five years after I went to Vietnam to help contain the Chinese communists—who were, remember, according to our government, supporting and directing the Viet Cong—President Richard Nixon stood on the Great Wall of China with Communist Premier Chou En Lai, smiling and shaking hands while American GIs continued to fight and die in the mud and muck of Indochina.

Consider this: eight years after I went to Vietnam to prevent the Domino Theory from tumbling into San Diego, the fall of South Vietnam to the communists was reported on the six o'clock news with hardly more impact than the story of a bad fire in Cleveland. The lives of Americans were not altered in any way. Kids continued to play ball in the park, mothers and fathers went to work, and all America geared up feverishly for the coming bicentennial celebration.

Consider this: when the *Pentagon Papers*—the government's own history of the war in Vietnam—became public, they revealed a stark, willful pattern of deception, misrepresentation and outright lies on the part of U.S. policymakers regarding the situation in Vietnam and the U.S. government's intentions over the entire course of the war.

But that was Vietnam; that's ancient history. What does it have to do with you? Consider how the United States has dealt with the people responsible for the Vietnam war. McGeorge Bundy, whom the *Pentagon Papers* identifies as the major architect of U.S. policy in Vietnam, became president of the Ford Foundation. Robert S. McNamara, Secretary of Defense under Presidents Kennedy and Johnson, became president of the World Bank. General William C. Westmoreland, who built up U.S. troop levels from 30,000 to

500,000, insisting all the while that he could see the light at the end of the tunnel, was promoted to Army Chief of Staff. Harold Brown, who as secretary of the Air Force called for extensive bombing of North Vietnam with the deliberate intention of inflicting civilian damage and civilian casualties, was appointed Secretary of Defense by President Carter. Paul H. Nitze, a senior official in the Defense Department during the war, was appointed chief U.S. negotiator for strategic arms limitations talks by President Reagan.

In short, the people who got us into Vietnam and kept us there for a quarter of a century have continued to be and still are an integral part of the policy-making apparatus of the U.S. government. President Reagan himself has repeatedly called the U.S. war in Indochina "a noble cause."

Now consider the fates of those of us who actually fought in that noble cause. There are approximately 2.5 million of us. Forty-eight thousand of us were killed in combat. Another 10,000 of us died in Vietnam of non-combat incidents. More than 300,000 of us were wounded in action, including 21,000 permanently physically disabled. Thirteen thousand of us were diagnosed as permanently disabled due to psychological or neurological disorders.

All through the decade of the 1970s, responsible medical authorities indicated repeatedly that one-third to one-half of all Vietnam veterans suffered chronic psychological problems resulting from the war. By 1976, 500,000 of us had attempted suicide since coming home. Fifty-five thousand of us succeeded in that tragic attempt, or died of drug overdose or in single-car accidents. Yet it was not until 1979 — 17 years after the first of us were sent to Vietnam, six years after the last of us came home — that the United States government even acknowledged psychological trauma as a Vietnam-related injury and the Veterans Administration began to treat those of us with stress problems. And every year since Reagan's election in 1980, funding for those Vietnam Veterans Outreach Clinics has gotten smaller and smaller.

Consider that the jobless rate among Vietnam veterans has continued to be among the highest in the country, while the GI Bill that was supposed to enable us to go to college turned out to be hardly enough to pay for our books. Consider that Vietnam veterans have the highest divorce rate in the nation, and that as early as 1973, 32 percent of all inmates in federal prisons were Vietnam veterans. Consider that in 1980, Vietnam veterans were honored on a U.S. postage stamp, but the U.S. government still refuses to treat most Vietnam veterans afflicted with symptoms of Agent Orange poisoning, contracted by exposure to the chemical defoliants used by U.S. forces in Vietnam. And consider that those of us who tried to tell our fellow citizens what was really happening in Vietnam were characterized by Vice President of the United States Spiro T. Agnew as "malcontents, radicals, incendiaries, civil and uncivil disobedients, yippies, hippies, yahoos, Black Panthers, lions and tigers."

And all of this has a great deal to do with you because you are the next potential crop of American war veterans. You, or your boyfriends and brothers and husbands and cousins and friends. Consider the recruiting ads current on television these days that proclaim in slick technicolor: "The Few, the Proud, the Marines"; "Air Force—a great way of life"; "The Navy: it's not just a job; it's an adventure"; "Be all you can be in today's Action Army."

Consider that the U.S. government maintains that the guerrilla movement in El Salvador is the brainchild of the Russians and the baby of the Cubans—an argument almost identical to the claims made about Vietnam twenty years ago—and this in spite of the fact that a former U.S. ambassador to El Salvador has characterized the president of the Salvadoran National Assembly as "a pathological killer." Consider that the present administration has created the largest increase in the military budget since the Second World War, and intends to double that increase by 1985. Consider that the United States is the world's largest exporter of arms and armaments. Now consider again President Reagan's changing position on draft registration.

I can't possibly tell you here all that I would like to tell you—all that I have learned in the 16 years since I sat where you are now sitting. But I can tell you a few things. I still believe that all of us owe something to our country, but I am no longer convinced that what I owe my country is military service whenever and wherever my government demands it. Furthermore, if I owe something to my country, my country also owes something to me—and to each one of you: it owes us the obligation not to ask for our lives unless it is absolutely necessary. And I believe absolutely that in the course of my lifetime and yours, the U.S. government—regardless of the particular administration or political party in power—has failed that obligation time and time again.

I will not tell you to become conscientious objectors, or to urge your friends and brothers and boyfriends to become conscientious objectors. But I sincerely hope that all of you will begin now to learn the things that I failed to learn until it was too late, to question beliefs and assumptions I failed to question until the damage had been done.

I hope that none of you will ever have to face the kind of decision that I faced when I was your age. But if you do, I hope even more that you will be able to look back on your decision and honestly conclude that you made the right choice. Because you will have to live with that decision for the rest of your lives — if you live at all — and I can tell you from hard experience that the wrong choice is an awesome burden indeed.

WAITING FOR THE FIRE

Just about the time Walter Lowenfels was gathering his anthology of antiwar protest poems, *Where Is Vietnam?*, I was going through Marine Corps boot camp. I didn't have to ask where Vietnam was; I knew perfectly well that it was just down the road: a mile marker on the communist highway to San Diego. I'd turned down four colleges to volunteer for the war, and I had no use for Lowenfels and his peacenik fellow-travelers.

Oh, I liked poetry well enough. In high school, I'd read Stephen Crane and Walt Whitman, Rudyard Kipling, Carl Sandburg and Wilfred Owen. I knew that war is kind, and it's Tommy this and Tommy that, and the grass covers all. But I also knew my duty. Moreover, with that blind eagerness possessed only by the young, I genuinely looked forward to the exultation, fellowship, and merriment Owen had promised in "Apologia Pro Poemate Meo."

Once in Vietnam, however, I was quickly disabused of my romantic notions. And I came home in a rage of confusion and hurt — not to the parades and accolades I had imagined as a child, but to a country that didn't seem to want to hear that all I'd done was kill people who had never done me any harm.

One might think that the experience would have made me look a little more kindly upon the likes of Lowenfels and company, but it didn't happen that way. Instead, I traded one kind of blindness for another. The few poems I read about Vietnam after I came back only made me angry. What the hell did these people know about it, for chrissake?! When *Poetry* published its special issue on Vietnam, all I registered was that it didn't include one single poem by a Vietnam veteran.

53

For a long time, in fact—longer than I care to admit—I really believed that you couldn't write about Vietnam unless you'd been there. It was the credo of a sore loser, both as veteran and poet, but I clung to it tenaciously. Then one day in late 1975, I happened upon Philip Appleman's "Waiting for the Fire," and his lucid description of Vietnam and its aftermath struck me with the force of authority:

> Not just the temples, lifting
> lotuses out of the tangled trees,
> not the moon on cool canals,
> the profound smell of the paddies,
> evening fires in open doorways,
> fish and rice the perfect end of wisdom;
> but the small bones, the grace, the voices like
> clay bells in the wind, all wasted.

It is a beautiful and heartbreaking poem in its entirety, and it captured the way I was feeling just then as I hadn't thought possible of an "outsider." And the shock of that discovery was followed soon after by the equally shocking discovery of W. S. Merwin's "The Asians Dying." My God, I thought as I read it, this guy knows what I had been, and been a part of, as though he had been a part of it himself:

> Like columns of smoke they advance into the shadows
> Like thin flames with no light
> They with no past
> And fire their only future[.]

The two poems went a long way toward teaching me that people other than Vietnam veterans might have something worthwhile to say about Vietnam.

That might not seem like a startling revelation to most people, but it was to me. For the first time since I'd come home from the war, I began to understand that the tragedy of Vietnam had touched not just the suckers and the triggermen in the rice fields, but the entire nation—including, of course, its poets. Daniel Hoffman once told me that "poems on public subjects can only be real when the public subject has become a private, personal subject in some way." And the Vietnam war found a multitude of ways to make itself private and personal.

The media—television in particular—played a major role in

fostering that sense of the private and personal in people who might otherwise have escaped the war unscathed. Certainly, for instance, the suppression of the Filipino independence movement had been every bit as brutal as the attempted suppression of the Vietnamese independence movement. But there had been no immediacy to the Philippine war; Americans hadn't had to see with their own eyes what the Blessings-of-Civilization had meant to Filipinos.

More than half a century later, however, the war in Vietnam came into every livingroom in the United States—day after day, year after agonizing year. Perhaps for the first time in history, the citizenry of a dominant power witnessed almost first-hand the crushing weight of empire and the roots of its foundation.

That seemed to produce two simultaneous effects. Firstly, it generated uncomfortable historical analogies that demanded introspection. Marge Piercy's "The Peaceable Kingdom" likens Lyndon Johnson to a Roman Caesar, and Appleman's "Peace with Honor" convincingly sustains the Roman analogy for an entire poem. Howard Nemerov's "On Getting Out of Vietnam" draws upon ancient Mycenae. In "The Inductees on the Plane," David Ray notices that the medals worn by young soldiers are "Maltese crosses/Like the ones the Nazis wore." And Wendell Berry's "Dark with Power" starkly conjures the conquerors of all the ages:

> Pray to us, farmers and villagers
> of Vietnam. Pray to us, mothers
> and children of helpless countries.
> Ask for nothing.

Secondly, massive media exposure generated a powerful empathy with the people on the receiving end of the war. Day after day, Americans watched Vietnamese—and it was obvious that they were human beings who were suffering greatly. "Think of the children there," writes Hayden Carruth in "The Birds of Vietnam," "insane little crusted kids at the beckoning fire." Galway Kinnell, in "Vapor Trail Reflected in the Frog Pond," makes the media connection explicit: "TV groaning at the smells of the human body,/ curses of the soldier as he poisons, burns, grinds, and stabs/ the rice of the world." And a Buddhist monk "sat on the warm asphalt and touched the match" in Joseph Bruchac's "June Through September, 1963."

Moreover, it was not just empathy that was generated, but a frightening vision of "there-but-for-the-grace-of-God," a disturbing ability to perceive the war from the other end of the barrel. Writes Louis Simpson in "American Dreams":

> As I look down the street
> on a typical sunny day in California
> it is my home that is burning
> and my dear ones that lie in the gutter
> as the American army enters.

Hoffman, too, finds the public subject all too personal. In a marvelous poem called "A Special Train," he writes: "And, look, in this paddy/ A little boy is putting in the shoots./ He's naked in the sunlight. It's my son!"

Of course, there were many other ways in which the war became personal. Denise Levertov writes of a trip she took to Vietnam. Ray meets soldiers on an airplane, and years later, encounters Vietnamese refugee children in "Vietnam." Muriel Rukeyser's contact with young war resisters surfaces in "The Hostages." And younger poets had to deal with the draft and the knowledge that it was their peers in Vietnam. Christopher Bursk writes, in "Adjust, Adjust," of the helplessness he feels:

> Coward, can't you die
> while wrists are cut, throats slit, children gassed in Vietnam? At twenty-four can you only cry while men shoot themselves to death in the DMZ[?]

And it's true, also, that many people — poets and others — opposed the war from the very beginning.

The end result of it all, however — long before the war ended — was to alienate vast numbers of people from their government, institutions, and political leadership, and often from long-held values as well. Observes Piercy, again in "The Peaceable Kingdom": "The rhetoric of the republic gilds empire." Or Richard Wilbur in "A Miltonic Sonnet for Mr. Johnson on His Refusal of Peter Hurd's Official Portrait": "Wait, Sir, and see how time will render you,/Who talk of vision but are weak of sight." For many Americans, the American Dream — the myth of the land of the free and the home of the brave — died in the rice fields and mangrove swamps of Vietnam. "The future, fabled bird," writes Levertov in "In Thai Binh (Peace) Province," "has migrated away from America[.]"

Those long, gut-wrenching years produced, among other things, a tremendous amount of poetry. And the anguish and frustration of those writers are as real and personal as anything experienced by the Vietnam veterans themselves, though the focus of the subject may differ. To make some kind of distinction between veterans and non-veterans is to set one group of victims against another—a tactic used by Richard Nixon with devastating effectiveness—and if it took me years to understand that, I understand it now.

In terms of the poetry, of course, what works and doesn't work is another matter. Robert Bly's often-anthologized "Asian Peace Offers Rejected Without Publication," though admirable in intent, falls flat because he never tells one *why* "Men like [Dean] Rusk are not men,/[but rather] bombs waiting to be loaded in a darkened hangar." I know why—but the high school students I now teach don't; it has to be in the poem, not in the reader's head. Likewise, Allen Ginsberg's "Pentagon Exorcism" assumes too much. Most of Rukeyser's Vietnam poetry fails to provide its own context. And Levertov's "What Were They Like?" lacks depth of feeling and the power present in "In Thai Binh (Peace) Province."

But many of the poems do work—some of them, like "Waiting for the Fire" and "The Asians Dying," spectacularly. Moreover, I find I have to respect the poems that don't work almost as much as the ones that do. Not long ago, I found myself trying to write a poem about El Salvador and the growing trouble there. I've never been there, and I don't know much about it. But what I do know bothers me deeply. So there I was, thrashing around on the paper, and I suddenly realized that this must have been the very predicament in which the writers I've been discussing found themselves ten and fifteen years ago. The years had come around to me at last.

I expect the poem I finally ended up with isn't much, but I felt compelled to say what I could, and if nothing else, it's an honest poem. Surely the poems in *Where Is Vietnam?* were equally honest, their authors equally compelled. And if those and similar poems had no impact on me until years later, it says less about the poems than it does about why armies are always made up of the young. In a world forever mad, and now facing extinction, it is and always has been the duty of thoughtful people to do what little they can to hold back the fire.

PRESERVING THE
AMERICAN MYTH

The cover of Stanley Karnow's *Vietnam: A History* heralds the book as "The First Complete Account of Vietnam at War." Unfortunately, the book fails to live up to that claim. Not only is it incomplete, but it is riddled with distortions, half-truths and outright lies.

Karnow, who served as chief correspondent for the Public Television series *Vietnam: A Television History* (to which this book is a companion), gets the book off to a very poor start by titling the first chapter "The War Nobody Won," ignoring the fact that for the first time in 100 years Vietnam is both unified and free of foreign domination. Once he begins writing, he goes rapidly from bad to worse.

Consider, for instance, his analysis of U.S. history during the late 19th and early 20th centuries. Contrasting the United States with the various European powers "who were then carving up Asia and Africa," Karnow explains that "there was little inclination in America for dominating foreign territories." He does mention in passing that the U.S. did happen to acquire Hawaii, Guam, Samoa, Puerto Rico, Cuba and the Philippines, but quickly points out that "as former rebels against oppressive British colonialism, Americans were instinctively repelled by the idea of governing other peoples."

Apparently uneasy with his own contradictory evidence, however, he then goes on to explain that "Cuba was granted independence" and "the Philippines were scheduled for eventual autonomy." He does not mention the Platt Amendment, forced

58

upon the Cubans at gunpoint by the U.S. government, which made a mockery of Cuban independence for the next sixty years. Nor does he mention that the Philippines had to wait half a century for "eventual autonomy." Nor does he mention the remarkably sordid chain of events which led to U.S. acquisition of Hawaii. Nor does he mention that Guam, Samoa and Puerto Rico are still essentially U.S. colonies. He does mention, though, that the U.S. "characteristically used an indemnity fund for damages incurred during the Boxer uprising [in China] to school Chinese in the United States."

Moving on, he then describes in vivid detail the economic hardships faced by Vietnam today. The blame for this he lays squarely on the heads of the current regime, which, he claims, "committed blunders that ruined their chances of winning the peace." And what blunders did they commit? "In 1977, Pham Van Dong and his comrades squandered an opportunity to establish diplomatic ties with the United States. Secretary of State Cyrus Vance and one of his chief aides, Richard Holbrooke, were keen to grant American recognition to Vietnam as a step toward reconciliation, and President Jimmy Carter favored the move." A feeler was extended, claims Karnow, but the Vietnamese failed to act on it, thus missing the opportunity to cash in on American largesse and get their economy back on its feet.

All of this Karnow delivers with no suggestion that the severe economic difficulties facing Vietnam since the end of the war might have anything at all to do with thirty years of war forced upon a poor agrarian society, first by the French with U.S. approval and eventual massive support, and later directly by the Americans. Nor is there any mention that this single diplomatic feeler—if it indeed ever occurred at all—took place in the midst of a welter of clearly and openly hostile signals and actions, as though the Vietnamese were somehow by divine inspiration supposed to be able to grasp this one straw in a haystack of hatred and animosity, cling to it, and thereby be saved from their current economic woes. But no, says Karnow, the "inept" and "incompetent" Vietnamese leaders inexplicably missed their one big chance, so it's not the fault of the United States if Vietnam still suffers from the ravages of three decades of war.

One could go on and on, but these few examples should suffice. Of such fantastic logic and historical distortion is "objective" history composed. The clear and final conclusion Karnow moves toward is that the poor, naïve, good-hearted Americans stumbled into a sad series of well-intentioned mistakes, but the cause was nevertheless just, the enemy without morality or conscience, and the Vietnamese are far worse off today than they would have been if we had somehow managed to win.

What makes this book not just a bad book but a dangerous one is that most Americans will be more than willing to accept those conclusions. Americans can deal with leaders who make mistakes—even enormous ones—with the best of intentions. What most of us can't deal with—can't even begin to conceive of, in fact—is the vision of the United States as a source of evil in the world every bit as malignant as that arch-villain, the Soviet Union. Such a notion runs against the very fabric of self-perception. It is too hideous to imagine.

And so we turn away from that terrible vision and seek solace in explanations like Karnow's which offer us a less painful way of explaining the havoc we sow in the world. And Karnow, for all of the embarrassing facts he reveals, makes it plain that we're still, after all, the seat of liberty and justice, the beacon of hope in a world threatened by communist domination and repression. We failed to save the Vietnamese from themselves, but perhaps we'll succeed in Central America.

GOING BACK

Nguyen Thi Na is 67 years old. She lives in a small hamlet in Cu Chi District, 35 kilometers west of the city that was once called Saigon. Her simple brick house was built for her only a few years ago by the People's Committee of Cu Chi, the Vietnamese equivalent of a county government. As I approach the house, half a dozen small children playing nearby at first stop and stare, then giggle nervously and scurry out of sight. Dao Van Duc, vice president of the People's Committee, takes my arm gently and gestures for me to enter the house.

Inside, I bow uneasily to Mrs. Na and take a seat across the table from her. The walls are bare, except for a row of five identical certificates, framed in black and trimmed in red and yellow. I recognize the seal of the Socialist Republic of Vietnam on each certificate, but cannot read the words, which are Vietnamese. Mr. Duc begins to introduce me, but before he has finished, Mrs. Na's eyes are brimming with tears.

"I gave all five of my sons to the Revolution," she says through an interpreter, her toothless mouth trembling with the effort to maintain control of her voice, "and all five of them are dead." She gestures sharply to the five certificates hanging above her head. "I have suffered so much misery—and you did this to me."

She does not say: the Americans did this. She does not say: you Americans did this. "*You* did this to me," she says. It is uncanny, almost as if she can see me as I once was: a young American Marine slogging through flooded paddy fields, armed to the teeth, frightened and mean. The wrinkled leathery skin of her face crinkles into a grimace, and the tears begin to fall onto the bare wood of the

61

table between us. And I can only sit in stunned silence, dizzy from heat and shock.

Somewhere in the murky haze of my mind, words are moving— lines from a poem I wrote over ten years ago called "Making the Children Behave":

> Do they think of me now
> in those strange Asian villages
> where nothing ever seemed
> quite human
> but myself
> and my few grim friends
> moving through them
> hunched
> in lines?

> When they tell stories to their children
> of the evil
> that awaits misbehavior,
> is it me they conjure?

A decade later, I finally have my answer. I want to get up and walk out into the hot dusty afternoon and throw up in the road. I want to be home in bed with my wife's arms wrapped warmly around me. Why have I put myself deeply into debt and traveled halfway around the world just to confront a reality more terrible than imagination? What can I say to this lonely old woman who already knows what I am? This is not what I wanted, I think vaguely as another wave of nausea washes over me; this is not it at all.

What I wanted was a great catharsis, a personal healing that would finally allow me to put the demons to bed and get on with my life. I had gone to Vietnam in February 1967 as an 18-year-old Marine volunteer. I had served 13 months in an infantry battalion in central Vietnam. I had been wounded in battle, decorated, and promoted. Indeed, I had been a model Marine, earning the rank of sergeant long before my 20th birthday. But along the way, directly and indirectly, I had wreaked havoc upon the people of Vietnam.

Eventually I came to my own conclusions, and I've been able to live with them. But the memories of Vietnam at war, and my complicity in that war, have never left me. For years I have wanted to go back. To walk along paddy dikes without fear of mines. To stroll through the streets of Hue that I had once helped to fill with rubble and bodies. To see green rice growing on that filthy lump of mud and barbed wire up along the Demilitarized Zone called Con Thien. I felt certain that if I could only see the Vietnamese getting on with their lives, the war gone and the awful wreckage of war grown over and forgotten, I too would be able to let go.

It is no easy task to travel to Vietnam. Ten years after the end of the war, the United States government still maintains an openly hostile posture toward the new regime—a kind of institutionalized sour grapes. There are no diplomatic relations between the two countries, which makes it difficult and complicated to obtain a visa. But in spite of the obstacles, after four long years of false starts and dead ends, in December 1985 I finally found myself aboard a Russian-built Air Laos turboprop, crossing over the Red River and descending toward Hanoi. Below me, I could see oxen and water buffalo, thatch-roofed huts, and dry ricefields distinctly separated by those once-terrifying dikes. Scattered among the fields and houses were the pockmarks of craters left behind by American bombers fully 13 years earlier.

In the city of Hanoi, one notices first the bicycles—thousands of them clogging every road and street. In a country where spare parts are scarce and fuel is at a premium, bikes have long since become the workhorses of everyday life. There were bicycles piled eight feet high with cordwood. Bikes with three four-foot-high earthen jars strapped to the rear wheel and fender. Pedicabs—called cyclos. Tricycle trucks. Bikes loaded with baskets of potatoes or coal. Bikes with one, two and three people aboard. Twenty years ago, when the Ho Chi Minh Trail was nothing but a series of rough tracks in the jungle, the North Vietnamese Army used bicycles to haul everything from ammunition to medical supplies 1,000 miles through a rain of American bombs to the battlefields of the south. So this is how they did it, I thought as the impossible stampede of bicycles swarmed all around me.

Trucks and cars are scarce in Hanoi. Most cars in Vietnam are old, repaired and jury-rigged many times over, and stripped of almost every accessory. Except the horn, of course. It is not possible to navigate around the bicycles without a horn. One starts the engine and the horn simultaneously, and the horn is never silent until the engine stops running. Still, cars, trucks and bicycles seem

remarkably considerate of each other. To look at the apparent confusion on the roads, one cannot help wondering how the Vietnamese avoid strewing bodies all over the place. But in sixteen
days, I saw only two minor accidents, neither involving a motor
vehicle or physical injury.

But I had hardly arrived when I was told that I would not be able
to visit a single place that I had served in. There had been a severe
typhoon in the Hue area, I was informed by my hosts, the Commission for Investigation into War Crimes—the worst in 40 years.
Travel to Hue would be impossible, my hosts told me. I couldn't
believe what I was hearing. What about Danang, I asked. Hoi An?
Con Thien? No, I was told; they were very sorry, but it was
impossible.

That first night, alone in my room in the Unification Hotel (the
Metropole in the days of the French), the enormity of the news
sank in. What did Hanoi matter to me? Or Saigon (now called Ho
Chi Minh City)? My friends had died in places called Hieu Nhon
and Dien Ban. I had lost my youth in places called Ai Tu and
Phuoc Trac. I needed to see those places again, to see children
playing and old men tending water buffalo on the once-bloody soil
upon which I'd nearly died. I had dreamed of those places for years,
and I had come a long way physically and emotionally to see them.

I stretched out on the bed only to discover that a permanent sag
in the mattress hurled me automatically into a tight fetal ball. Bit-
terly disappointed, I became acutely aware of the shabbiness that
surrounded me. The single naked lightbulb hanging from the ceiling. The cracked plaster on the walls. The missing tiles in the
bathroom. The missing knob on the closet. The toilet down the
hall that wouldn't flush. I did not want to be here. What would I
do for the next two weeks? It is hard for a man of 37 to have to
come to terms with his own foolish romanticism.

But there was nothing for it but to get up the next morning and
go on. My hosts had planned a full schedule for me, and there was
no use trying to explain that I wasn't interested. Over the next few
days, I was whisked from one meeting to the next: briefings with
General Tran Kinh Chi, vice president of the commission, the
Kampuchean embassy, the Hanoi Friendship and Solidarity Committee, the Vietnam–U.S. Society, the Central Committee for

Vietnamese Culture, Literature and Art, the Writers' Union, the Palace of Children, Bach Mai Hospital, the Museum of History, the Nguyen Viet Xuan School for War-Orphaned Children. I met more people, drank more coffee and tea, smoked more Dien Bien cigarettes, and ate more bananas and tangerines than I can ever begin to recount.

And a funny thing happened: in spite of my bitter personal disappointment, I began to get interested.

Van Mieu Pagoda—the Temple of Literature—was the first university in Vietnam. Founded in 1077, it operated continuously for eight centuries. Now it is preserved as a museum and cultural shrine. "Literature is as necessary as the sunshine," says the middle-aged woman who is curator. "On that balcony there, the poets used to come to read their poems to the people." She reaches into her pocket and comes up with a small enamel pin with the Poets' Balcony painted on it. "I want you to have this," she says. "When the Americans were here before, they bombed us. I'm glad you've come to the Temple of Literature. I'm very glad to meet you."

"Do you remember the bombing?" I ask Duong Van Loan, my 25-year-old interpreter/guide.

"Yes," she replies, "it was terrible." She explains that she and most other children of Hanoi were evacuated to the countryside in 1965. For seven years, she lived with her grandparents, seeing her parents only once each week. "We were close enough to hear the sirens and the guns and the bombs exploding. When the raids finally stopped, we were so happy that we ran all the way back to the city."

Te Hanh, age 65, is one of Vietnam's two most respected living poets. He looks like a poet, with slightly disheveled thin gray hair and keen eyes. Though I never can get a straight answer about censorship and state control of publishing, we talk for several hours about poetry and the relationship of art to life. When I show him my poem, "Making the Children Behave," he becomes very excited. Quickly flipping through an anthology, he points to a poem of his called "Questions Underground":

When there are no more bombs,
Shall you let me go up on the earth again?
I want to see again the uncles and aunts I loved.

Are they still fighting, Mama?
I want to see the Yankee,
Mama; does it look like a human being?

Nguyen Van Hung, 38, is missing his right arm from the shoulder. We are sitting next to each other at a small dinner sponsored by the director of a radio and television repair factory, a sturdy woman in her late forties with advanced degrees in electrical engineering. The factory hires only war orphans and disabled veterans. As we talk, Mr. Hung and I discover that both of us fought in Hue during the Tet Offensive of 1968, and a kind of brotherhood of adversaries takes root between us.

"You weren't a B-40 gunner, were you?" I ask with a laugh, wondering if by some eerie coincidence this might be the man who wounded me.

"No," he replies, "I was with the special units. I was a sapper"—a demolitions engineer.

I wonder why I like this man. I lost so many friends to men like him. But then, how many friends did he lose to men like me? It was all so long ago, and we were very young.

"Did you lose your arm in Hue?" I ask.

"No," he explains, "I lost it near the Laotian border in 1971." My war lasted 13 months. His lasted until he was physically dismembered. He smiles at me, fascinated by my ability to roll cigarettes by hand, and asks me to roll one for him. When the dinner ends, he takes my hand in his and squeezes it. "I'm glad you weren't killed," he says. He breaks into a broad toothy grin, and for some reason that I cannot explain, I embrace him with both arms, happy that both of us have lived to share this moment.

In the center of Hanoi lies Restoration Sword Lake. In the middle of the lake lies an island upon which stands Jade Hill Pagoda, built to honor the memory of Tran Hung Dao, a 13th century Vietnamese general who defeated Chinese invaders. China has invaded Vietnam repeatedly over the course of the past four millennia, at one point occupying Vietnam for nearly 1,000 years. More recent intrusions by France, Japan and the United States are mere aberrations in the great sweep of Vietnamese history.

"China is our natural enemy," General Kinh Chi has said in one of his briefings—and the imposition of communist governments in both countries has not altered that ancient antagonism, as the ongoing border war between the two countries attests. If only American policymakers had taken the time to learn what every Vietnamese schoolchild knows, how very different might have been the course of the past 40 years.

In 1077, on the eve of yet another battle against Chinese invaders, the Vietnamese general Ly Thuong Kiet wrote this poem:

> Over the mountains and rivers of Vietnam reigns the Emperor
>   of Vietnam,
> As it stands written in the Book of Heaven.
> How is it that you strangers dare to invade our land?
> Your armies, without pity, shall be annihilated.

The curator of the Museum of History tells me that Le Duc Tho recited this poem to Henry Kissinger during the course of the Paris Peace Conference.

The mausoleum of Ho Chi Minh is an elegantly simple building rising from the middle of a large public square. To enter the tomb, you line up by twos several hundred yards from the building and walk down a red carpet to the entrance, escorted by a uniformed army officer. As you get close to the entrance, the pace of the officer slows to a solemn funereal walk. Inside, up several flights of stairs, you enter a room where the body of Bac Ho — Uncle Ho — lies quietly in a glass case, flanked by four armed soldiers standing at attention. You are allowed to stand and look for perhaps a minute, then you are ushered out.

Throughout Vietnam, Ho Chi Minh has been elevated to the status of a secular god. His photograph, his bust, and his face are everywhere. To a foreign observer, it is almost as if no other soul ever contributed one iota to Vietnamese independence in the 20th century. Nevertheless, in Vietnam, one does not have to be a Marxist-Leninist to revere him. During the war, we often came upon houses with small altars to Ho. The people in those houses were usually beaten and arrested, the houses often destroyed. We were told that Ho Chi Minh was a communist. No one ever told us that many Vietnamese, both northerners and southerners, hold him in much the same esteem as we hold George Washington. How many Viet Cong did our blundering ignorance produce?

Hanoi is a poor city in a poor country. There are some new buildings to be seen, both residential and public, but most of the city was built by the French before World War Two, and even the newer buildings seem coated with a perpetual sheen of dust. There are few streetlights, the traffic lights have long since ceased to work, and a good cyclo driver can easily outrun the old French trolleys. Yet poverty is not a word that seems appropriate.

I walked alone through the streets of Hanoi for many hours and many miles during my week there. Though I had to register with the police upon my arrival, most nights and some afternoons I was free to come and go wherever my feet would take me. I stumbled upon a Buddhist pagoda where saffron-robed monks sat busily studying what appeared to be old manuscripts, and a Catholic cathedral where several hundred people sat chanting the rosary. Few people were bold enough to ask me where I was from, and without my interpreter communication was often difficult and haphazard. Some people seemed to assume I was Russian; they would look at me and say the word for "Soviet." When I'd reply "My"—American—they often seemed surprised, even amused, but quickly turned away and went about their business, as if to stare too long would be impolite.

In the older section of the city, called Old Hanoi, the narrow streets are clogged with small shops and women selling cabbage, potatoes, grapefruit and pineapple. Streetside vendors sell pâté sandwiches and sweet drop-donuts. Young off-duty soldiers are everywhere, but armed police are unobtrusive and armed soldiers even more rare. One afternoon, I watched two young men shaping a massive roof beam with an ancient two-handled saw while another man hauled bricks in a beat-up sawed-off 55-gallon drum.

How does one describe it? There was a palpable spirit to these people of Hanoi, a kind of pride and strength that was real and undeniable. Reluctant to walk alone at night in my own neighborhood back home, I felt no fear strolling through Hanoi—even late at night, lost amid the tiniest, dirtiest back alleys of Old Hanoi. Poor as they are, I saw no old men curled up at night on park benches, no bag ladies. And no one begs. What I remember most is a small boy sitting beneath a banyan tree by the edge of the lake reading a book. He looked up at me for a moment, smiling, then returned to his story.

By the time I boarded the Air Vietnam turboprop for the flight to Ho Chi Minh City, I wasn't feeling so badly about not getting to visit the places where I'd actually been stationed. In fact, I was even feeling a bit ashamed of myself: after all, here was a poor nation struggling against enormous odds — and I had been pouting because I couldn't play out my private little fantasy. Surely I could afford to be more generous than that. Still, as the plane flew over central Vietnam and I strained unsuccessfully to see the earth through the thick cloud cover, a small piece of my heart got left behind, suspended in the air above the clouds.

Once one of the busiest airports in the world, Tan Son Nhut is now hardly a shadow of its former self. Dozens of old concrete revetments stand empty, and tall grass grows up through the cracks at the edge of the tarmac. In one corner of the field is an aircraft graveyard filled with the rusting stripped-down hulks of American C-47s, C-123s and C-130s.

Physical differences between north and south are immediately apparent. Much of the older French architecture has been supplanted by newer American-style buildings. Though one could hardly say that motor vehicles are numerous, compared to Hanoi, Ho Chi Minh City is a madhouse of buses, three-wheeled Lambrettas, motorbikes and motorscooters — all whizzing along amid the more familiar crush of bicycles. Pollution control devices are unheard of, and the air reeks with the acid sting of burnt fumes. At the Nine Dragons Hotel (once the Frenchified and aristocratic Majestic), I discover that the toilet is in the bathroom rather than down the hall, and the air conditioning works. From the top floor of the hotel, one is afforded a spectacular view of the great ox-bow that gives the Saigon River its name: "Bend in the River."

I am startled to discover that the war crimes exhibit in Ho Chi Minh City contains as much material about post-liberation Chinese crimes and the crimes of Pol Pot as it does about the long American war. Once again, I am reminded that we were hardly more than a brief interlude in the ancient struggle of the Vietnamese against their giant northern neighbor.

My guide through the exhibit, a woman of about my age named Thieu Thi Tao, had been a Viet Cong agent and student activist during the war, she tells me. Arrested by the Saigon regime in 1968 at the age of 18, she spent six years in prison, including three years in the infamous Tiger Cages of Con Son prison island. She appears healthy enough, even slightly plump. She speaks in a soothing voice and has a charming smile. But she walks with a noticeable limp that causes her graceful ao dai — the beautiful traditional dress of Vietnamese women — to ripple awkwardly.

"Sometimes, a kind jailer would give us a bit of meat or fish," she says. "One day, a jailer gave me a small hot pepper. It tasted good — sweet, like candy. Once they threw a phosphorous grenade into our cell, setting us on fire. Water wouldn't stop the burning, but I poured urine on myself and the acid in my urine put the fire out."

"How did you keep from going mad?" I ask.

"I pretended to be far away," she replies, smiling. "They couldn't lock up my imagination. I knew we would win." She goes on to explain that many of her former tormentors have been re-educated and are now free. She even met one of them one day, walking on the street.

"Doesn't it bother you?" I ask.

"If we do not have successful national reunification," she replies firmly, "history has taught us that we will end up as a province of China."

I am sitting alone having lunch in a small restaurant near the hotel. The man next to me asks where I'm from. When I say the United States, he smiles in surprise. I ask him where he learned English, and he tells me he studied English literature at the university in Saigon in 1973 and 1974. Now he is a translator of Russian documents. I ask him what he thinks of the new regime. He laughs softly — a short, choked sigh. "I don't get involved in politics," he replies. As I pay the bill, he leans over to me. "They will know I've been talking to you," he says. "When I get back to work, they will question me. I'll tell them I was helping you with the menu." He laughs again and shrugs his shoulders. "You tell me you are a writer," he says. "You will understand what I say, and what I don't say."

Xuan Giai is a frail old man barely five feet tall with gray hair and thick glasses, but his eyes are alive with youthful vitality. His left thumb is missing. The father of eight children, he joined Ho Chi

Minh's Viet Minh army in 1945. He was wounded once by the French, twice by the Americans. His oldest son was killed by American soldiers in the Central Highlands in 1965.

"You must miss your wife," he says as we eat dinner aboard a floating restaurant in the Saigon River.

"I do," I laugh. "These three weeks seem like an eternity."

"Once, during the French war," he says, "I was separated from my wife for nine years." There is no hint of irony or condescension in his voice.

"It must seem a little dull these days," I say, "after all those years of soldiering." He stares at me with a puzzled look. "You know, as awful as war is," I try to explain, "after all you've seen and done, doesn't it seem dull sometimes to live such a quiet life?"

"Oh, no," he replies quickly. "I did what was necessary, but I never liked it. Give me a hundred years of peace. A thousand years. I don't want any more war."

Later, as we walk back to the hotel, Mr. Giai takes my hand in his as casually as if I were his grandson. Such a curious and beautiful custom, this business of holding hands. Men and women, of course, seldom hold hands in public; it would be scandalous, a breach of social etiquette. But two men, or two women—then it is only a sign of friendship and affection.

The last time I was in Vietnam, we used to think that two men holding hands in public must be homosexuals. We were convinced that half the men in Vietnam were "queer." And we let them know it, often and rudely. No one—not the president of the United States nor the most junior lieutenant—ever bothered to tell us what holding hands really meant. I doubt that they even knew.

Midday. I am sitting in a nearly deserted coffeeshop when the owner, a middle-aged woman, sits down at the vacant table next to me. "You're American, aren't you?" she says in English. "I used to work for the Americans. I was a secretary. On the last day, I tried to get out, but there was too much shooting around the U.S. embassy. I lay in the gutter with two of my children all day, then I went home." She looks around furtively, as if afraid that someone might be watching. "Look out for the cyclo drivers," she says. "They're all secret police."

"Are you getting along okay now?" I ask.

She shrugs and frowns. "Very bad," she says. "This used to be a restaurant, but the new regime will only let me sell beer, coffee and tea. I want to get out. Can you help me?"

I look at her helplessly. Once again, her eyes scan the street quickly, darting this way and that. She gets up and comes back, handing me a letter. It is signed by a U.S. immigration official and says that she and her family have been accepted for the Orderly Departure Program. It is several years old. "I can't get an exit visa," she says.

"I don't know what I can do," I reply. I really don't. I leave the coffeeshop with a hollow feeling inside. Nguyen Van Thieu lives in wealthy seclusion in London. Nguyen Cao Ky owns a liquor store in southern California. Nguyen Ngoc Loan, the infamous police chief of Saigon, runs a restaurant in Alexandria, Virginia. The rich and the powerful got out. The junior lieutenants and faithful servants we left behind.

General Nguyen Huu Hanh spent 29 years in the Saigon army fighting the communists. At various times he held high staff positions, and served as a Corps commander in both II and III Corps. When the end came, he was the man who issued the order for the Saigon army to lay down its weapons. That single act probably saved thousands of lives. Now he works with the new regime as a member of the Fatherland Front. Why did he stay behind, I ask. "I was misinformed about communism," he explains. "I am not a communist, but this is my country and the important thing now is to get on with rebuilding it. My hope is that eventually the Vietnamese will adapt the Soviet model to suit Vietnamese conditions and realities.

"After World War Two," he continues, "we thought the United States would help us gain independence." Instead, he says, U.S. military and civilian advisors "decided everything. They wouldn't listen to us. They had all the answers." Once, he tells me, when he was commander of II Corps, the famous American advisor John Paul Vann ordered him to replace one of his most senior lieutenants with a man of Vann's choosing. General Hanh thought Vann was wrong. "He threatened to cut off U.S. aid," says General Hanh, "and I was forced to make the change."

Another time, a different U.S. advisor ordered General Hanh to call for B-52 strikes in a certain area. General Hanh flew over the area, and though he knew there were VC present, he determined that there were too many civilians in the target area. "I refused to call in B-52s," he says. He was subsequently relieved of his command, B-52s were called in, and soon afterwards the entire area — including the local Saigon army garrison — went over to the Viet Cong side.

Mr. Duc of the district People's Committee is standing in the middle of a vast sugarcane field, part of the Pham Van Coi state farm, in Cu Chi District. Throughout the war, the district was a major VC stronghold — and a free fire zone that was virtually leveled during the course of the war. "All this used to be an American base," he explains — but there is nothing to be seen now but sugarcane and peanuts and soybeans. As we stand by the road, an older man comes by on a bicycle and stops to say hello to Mr. Duc. Strapped to the bike is a green metal cylinder. "It's part of an American rocket," the man explains, pointing to the U.S. markings stamped into the metal. "I made it into a waterpump." Then he breaks into a broad grin. "I like it better as a waterpump," he laughs. "It's a very good waterpump."

We stop again along another road in the district, but the landscape here looks more like the moon. There are large craters everywhere, laid out as if in systematic rows. Some of them are full of stagnant water. The earth around them is rock-hard and barren of life, except for a few scrubby weeds. "B-52s," says Mr. Duc. "We're filling in the craters as fast as we can. But we have to haul earth from a long distance, and we have very little heavy equipment, so it all has to be done by manual labor."

Later Mr. Duc takes me to a recently completed irrigation project, and then to the district hospital, which is completing a new wing that will expand the facility from 100 to 150 beds. "Every village in the district now has a clinic," he explains proudly.

As we drive along the roads of Cu Chi, I begin to feel a strangely satisfying sense of deja vu for the first time since I've been here. Small houses alone amid green trees or clustered together in small groups. Teams of buffalo plowing the fields. Men and women laboriously threshing rice by hand. Graceful fishing nets perched on long bamboo poles above small waterways. This is the Vietnam I remember: rural, simple, almost eternal.

What's different is the absence of war, the absence of Americans and barbed wire and artillery, the whop-whop of chopperblades and the whine of jet fighters. This is what I came for. Never mind ideology or right or wrong. Half my life I have longed to witness peace in this land I have never been able to see in my mind's eye except in the midst of war. So what if it's Cu Chi instead of Hieu Nhon? Look at it, boy, I think to myself, take it all in. Remember this. The world continues. It is harvest time, and the threshing floors are dancing with rice. There are winners and there are losers, but the war is over.

But just when I am beginning to feel pretty good, Mr. Duc takes me to meet Mrs. Na, who lost all five of her sons in the war. "You did this to me," she says, and it all comes flooding back: "Guerrilla War,"

> It's practically impossible
> to tell civilians
> from the Viet Cong.
>
> Nobody wears uniforms.
> They all talk
> the same language,
> (and you couldn't understand them
> even if they didn't).
>
> They tape grenades
> inside their clothes,
> and carry satchel charges
> in their market baskets.
>
> Even their women fight,
> and young boys,
> and girls.
>
> It's practically impossible
> to tell civilians
> from the Viet Cong.
>
> After awhile,
> you quit trying.

I do not know what to say to Mrs. Na. As we walk back to the car, Doan Duc Luu, my young interpreter/guide here in the south, slips his arm firmly around my waist. "That was very hard for you, wasn't it?" he asks. I wonder if I look as sick as I feel.

"Yes," I reply, grateful for his understanding.

But by the time we meet Tran Thi Bich at the open pavilion commemorating the tunnels of Cu Chi, I'm feeling much better. The tunnels are famous. Beginning in 1965, the VC constructed over 320 kilometers of interconnecting honeycombs, ingeniously camouflaged and murderously booby-trapped. The Americans knew the tunnels existed, but were never able to discover more than a small portion of them. Some of the tunnels even ran under U.S. military installations.

"Sometimes we would scurry out of the tunnels inside your lines, plant mines in the helicopters, and run back to the tunnels without being detected," says Miss Bich, giggling almost playfully. Miss Bich grew up in the tunnels, living in them from age eight to age 18. There were schools, hospitals, kitchens and munitions factories in the tunnels—a whole functioning community. She was mostly used as a courier, she explains, transmitting messages from one post to another or gathering visual intelligence.

A small portion of the tunnels is still kept open as a kind of living museum, and General Kinh Chi insists that I go down. It is hot, dark and close inside, the tunnel twisting and turning, rising and descending, pitch black and horribly confining. I'm frightened, but Miss Bich keeps urging me forward. I grope along on hands and knees, my head scraping the ceiling. I follow the sound of her voice, desperately searching for the light at the end of the tunnel. How could people actually live down here year in and year out, I wonder, let alone wage war so effectively? No wonder they beat us.

Finally I reach the end and climb out through a narrow trapdoor. I'm sweating heavily, breathing hard, and quite chagrined to discover that I've traveled all of 50 yards. Miss Bich reaches down to offer me a hand up. Her red Communist Youth League pin catches the sun as she smiles and takes my hand. It is an odd feeling: taking the hand of this warm, friendly woman who only a decade ago was my enemy.

It isn't just the American architecture or the awful smog that makes Ho Chi Minh City different from Hanoi, or the fact that things are only 10 years rundown instead of 40. The kind of personal reserve and dignity one sensed in Hanoi is far less evident here. People are more brash. They call hello in English with a harsh edge to their voices, and many of them want to sell you something or take you somewhere in their cyclos or beg money from you.

The Saigon Cowboys are long gone—the street punks and draft evaders. So, too, to all appearances, are most of the prostitutes and honky-tonk saloons and drug dealers that pandered to off-duty American GIs, and the thousands of homeless street people and hustlers and beggars and war profiteers. By any measure, Ho Chi Minh City is a much safer and saner place than Saigon ever was during the war—and indeed, one can find more thugs and beggars on any given day in Philadelphia than I encountered in Ho Chi Minh City.

Still, Ho Chi Minh City is a small shock after the proud austerity of Hanoi. I am much more at ease out in the country amid the rice fields and irrigation ditches and twisting waterways. This is the Vietnam I remember, the one I had so much wanted to see. So I am glad for the chance to drive up to Tay Ninh Province one day. Tay Ninh, land of Black Widow Mountain and the once-vast Michelin rubber plantations. Home of that curious messianic religious sect, the Cao Dai, whose three saints are Victor Hugo, Sun Yat-sen, and the 16th century Vietnamese philosopher-poet Nguyen Binh Khiem.

It is a long, dusty drive made slower by two flat tires and a clogged fuel pump. In the U.S., such mechanical difficulties are often accompanied by angry people kicking fenders and cursing to high heaven. I am perpetually amazed at the grace and stoicism with which the Vietnamese accept these setbacks. They are a fact of life in a poor country, and there is no use getting upset about it. While we wait for the driver to make repairs, we sip fresh sugarcane juice at a roadside stand, or watch an old man tending ducks in a flooded paddyfield, or play with children who have abandoned school to gawk at the strange foreigner.

I had forgotten the dust of Vietnam. Powdery fine and six inches thick on the road to Tay Ninh. Seeping into your nostrils and under your fingernails, coating your clothes and clogging every pore in your body. There was a time when I thought that I would never be able to wash the dust of Vietnam from my skin. "A clear mind spreads like the wind," goes an ancient Vietnamese folk poem. "By the Lo waterfalls, free and high, you wash away the dust of life."

After the long drive to Tay Ninh City, everyone is lying down, resting, but I want to walk down to the river to take pictures. The committee's information officer says it is okay. I walk out to the main gate, and as I approach I smile at the young policeman standing guard. He smiles back, but steps into my path. I hold up my camera, point toward the river only a hundred yards away, and explain that I'm just going to take a few photos, I'll be right back, I've got permission. He doesn't understand a word of English, but as I step forward again, he firmly places one hand on my arm while the other hand goes down to the barrel of the AK-47 he is carrying over his shoulder combat-style.

For a moment, my temper rises. Hey, dude, I'm a free man, I think angrily, who the hell do you think you are? Then I realize the absurdity of what I am thinking. This isn't my country, and I don't make the rules. Besides he's got a loaded AK. I've been on the wrong end of those suckers before, and this time I'm armed only with an Olympus XA-2. I get no pictures of the river in Tay Ninh City.

The Pagoda of the Sleeping Buddha perches on a hillside high above the South China Sea on the outskirts of Vung Tau, 125 kilometers east of Ho Chi Minh City. The Buddha itself, reclining peacefully on its left side, is a massive figure perhaps 30 feet long and polished to a fine pink sheen. An old monk offers me three sticks of incense. Years before, I had written a poem called "Souvenirs":

> "Bring me back a souvenir," the captain called.
> "Sure thing," I shouted back above the amtrac's roar.
>
> Later that day,
> the column halted,
> we found a Buddhist temple by the trail.
> Combing through a nearby wood,
> we found a heavy log as well.
>
> It must have taken more than half an hour,
> but at last we battered in
> the concrete walls so badly
> that the roof collapsed.
>
> Before it did,
> I took two painted vases
> Buddhists use for burning incense.
>
> One vase I kept,
> and one I offered proudly to the captain.

I take the incense sticks and hold them while the old man lights them. Standing before the Buddha with the sticks pressed between my palms, I bow three times, then place the incense in a large painted vase. The old monk seems pleased that I know the ritual. As I turn to go, he begins to hammer on a large bronze bell with a wooden mallet. He is waking up the spirits to receive my prayers.

Nguyen Thi My Huong is 14 years old. She is white Amerasian. Her friend, Nguyen Ngoc Tuan, is 15. He is black Amerasian. I met them in the park across from the old National Assembly on my first night in Ho Chi Minh City, and we've struck up a kind of friendship. As the week has passed and I've seen more of the city and the surrounding countryside, I've actually been surprised to see so few Amerasians — no more than half a dozen, all but one hanging around each night near the hotels where westerners stay. Perhaps it is true, as General Kinh Chi has told me, that most Amerasians really have been successfully integrated into Vietnamese society. I don't know.

But these two are here sitting beside me on my last night in Vietnam, and I hurt because there is nothing I can do for them. Tuan is a handsome boy, and Huong is perhaps the most beautiful child I have ever seen. Shy and skittish at first, she has warmed up to me over the passing days, and when she smiles, one dimple forms on the right side of her face.

It is hard to communicate with these two children, but we do the best we can in broken English and Vietnamese. Huong tells me that she knows her father's name, that he wants her to come to America, that she has papers and will be leaving in four months.

"What is your father's name?" I ask.

"Tony," she replies.

"Do you know his last name?" I ask. She doesn't seem to understand what I mean. "Write his name for me," I say, holding out a pen and notepad. "ENTONISTONI," she writes laboriously in uneven block letters, and I know now that there are no papers and there is no father waiting eagerly to receive her. As she hands me back the pad and pen, she asks me why I am crying.

"I'll miss you," I tell her. In our half-dozen evenings together, neither child has asked me for anything. They are not beggars, at least not with me. At last, it is time to go. I hold out my hand to Tuan and he shakes it firmly. Then I extend it to Huong, but she does not take it. She looks down at her feet and says something in Vietnamese. Then she looks at me and smiles shyly.

"She wants you to give her a kiss," says Tuan.

Tran Kinh Chi joined the Viet Minh army in 1945. He met his wife in the army. At one time or another, all seven of his children served in the army. One is a colonel now. When General Kinh Chi was a young colonel, he was assigned to escort Colonel Christian de Castries, commander of the fallen French garrison at Dien Bien Phu, to Hanoi. "It was a difficult march," he says, "de Castries was sick, and I had to give him all of my own medicine. If he had died along the way," he laughs, "it would have been my backside."

General Kinh Chi is waiting for me in the hotel lobby on the morning I am to leave. As always, he is dressed in civilian clothing. He is no longer an active general. "When the country needs soldiers," he has told me, "we are soldiers. Then we go on to other things." He has brought his six-year-old grandson with him this morning, the oldest of four grandchildren. He is very proud of the boy, and like any doting grandparent, wants to show him off. Over the past 16 days, I have grown very fond of this man who has been a kind host and solicitous companion, full of humor and grace. It is hard to believe that in another time he might have killed me.

Then I think of Richard Nixon standing on the Great Wall of China, smiling and shaking hands with communist premier Chou En Lai even as American boys still died in the war that we were told was being fought to blunt Chinese expansionism. Perhaps a day will come when I will not have to feel the need to defend my affection for this man who was once my adversary. At the airport we embrace. Then he is gone. And then I am gone. Most of my fellow passengers are Vietnamese, Orderly Departure Program emigrants bound for new lives in France and the United States. There are always winners and losers.

One would want this story to end here, perhaps, but two days after my return home, I found out that even as I was being told that travel to central Vietnam was not possible, eight American veterans were walking the streets of Hue, chipping spent M-16 rounds from the walls of the Citadel and recalling old and bitter battles. What had gone wrong? Why had I been denied the opportunity for which I had waited so long? Was it proof-positive of wily communist perfidy, or merely some bureaucratic bungle my hosts were too embarrassed to acknowledge — or something else I haven't even thought of? Perhaps I will never know.

And perhaps it doesn't matter. Now when I think of Vietnam, I will not see in my mind's eye the barbed wire and the grim patrols and the violent death that always exploded without warning. Now I will see those graceful fishing boats gliding out of the late afternoon sun across the South China Sea toward safe harbor at Vung Tau, and the buffalo boys riding the backs of those great gray beasts in the fields along the road to Tay Ninh. Now I will not hear the guns, but rather the gentle rhythmic beat of rice stalks striking the threshing mats.

I do not think for a moment that all is well in Vietnam. I had not expected to find a socialist workers' paradise, and the effects of 80 years of colonial exploitation, 30 years of war, and 10 years of economic and diplomatic isolation were everywhere painfully evident, as was the austere presence of a government I can hardly feel too comfortable about. Along with my memories of Mr. Hung and Miss Bich and Mr. Giai, I will carry forever the kiss I received from Nguyen Thi My Huong.

But the Vietnamese have no corner on the market for hardship, and the world is full of governments I can't begin to approve of — many of them among the staunchest allies and clients of the United States of America. At least in Vietnam today, no one is dropping bombs or burning villages or defoliating forests, and what is taking place is not being done in my name or with my tax dollars, and no one is asking me to participate. It is their country, finally, and it is their business what they do with it. The Vietnamese have burdens of their own to bear; they have no need and no use for my anguish or my guilt. My war is over. It ended long ago.

I am far more concerned these days about the war my children may one day be asked or even ordered to fight. Over 20 years ago, Lyndon Johnson told us that if we didn't stop the communists in Vietnam, we would have to fight them on the sands of Waikiki. Things didn't work out the way we expected them to, but the hotels along the beach in Honolulu seem to be doing just fine. Now we are being told that if we don't stop the communists in Nicaragua, we will have to fight them in the streets of Brownsville,

Texas. How long will it be before my government sends my children off to wage war against the children of another Nguyen Thi Na? Old Mrs. Na, whose sons we traveled ten thousand miles to kill.

SOLDIER-POETS
OF THE VIETNAM WAR

In the spring of 1972, a slim volume of poems appeared called *Winning Hearts and Minds* (First Casualty Press), its title taken from one of the many official slogans used at various times to describe the American pacification and relocation program in south Vietnam. Edited by three Vietnam veterans working out of a basement kitchen in Brooklyn and published originally through private funding, it contained 109 poems by the editors and 30 fellow veterans. With some notable exceptions, they were artless poems, lacking skill and polish, but collectively they impacted with the force of a wrecking ball.

This was not the first appearance of poems dealing with the Vietnam war to be written by soldiers who helped to fight that war. But *Winning Hearts and Minds* quickly became a classic: the seminal anthology against which all future Vietnam war poetry would be judged.

"[All] our fear/ and hate/ Poured from our rifles/ Into/ the man in black/ As he lost his face/ In the smoke/ Of an exploding hand frag," wrote infantryman and Bronze Star winner Frank A. Cross, Jr. "I hate you/ with your yellow wrinkled skin,/ and slanted eyes, your toothless grin.../ Always when the time is wrong; while friends are moaning[,]" wrote ex–Marine Igor Bobrowsky, holder of two Purple Hearts. "I'm afraid to hold a gun now," wrote Charles M. Purcell, holder of the Vietnamese Cross of Gallantry, "What if I were to run amuck here in suburbia/ And rush out into the street screaming/ 'Airborne all the way!'/ And shoot the milkman."

Most of the poems in *Winning Hearts and Minds* are carried by raw emotion alone, and most of the soldier-poets were not really poets at all, but rather soldiers so hurt and bitter that they could not maintain their silence any longer. Some, however, stand out more sharply than others. Bobrowsky, Cross and Purcell contribute powerful poems. Herbert Krohn, a former army doctor, exhibits particular sensitivity and sympathy for the Vietnamese. In "Farmer's Song at Can Tho," he writes:

> What is a man but a farmer
> Bowels and a heart that sings
> Who plants his rice in season
> Bowing then to the river.
> I am a farmer and I know what I know.
> This month's harvest is tall green rice.
> Next month's harvest is hordes of hungry beetles.
> How can peace be in a green country?

Co-editor Jan Barry (the other two editors were Basil T. Paquet and Larry Rottmann), who had served in Vietnam back in the days when U.S. troops were still called advisors, speaks of earlier occupations by the French, Japanese, Chinese and Mongols in "In the Footsteps of Ghenghis Khan," but concludes:

> Unencumbered by history
> our own or that of 13th-century Mongol armies
> long since fled or buried
> by the Vietnamese
> in Nhatrang, in 1962, we just did our jobs[.]

Barry is perhaps the single most important figure in the emergence of Vietnam veterans' poetry, not only for his own pioneering poems, but especially for his tireless efforts to encourage and promote the work of others.

But the two most noteworthy poets in the collection are Paquet and Michael Casey. Of the dozen or so poems Paquet contributes, three or four must rank as among the very best Vietnam war poems ever written. Literate without being literary, Paquet was, at the time, far and away the most skillful and practiced of the soldier-poets. His "Morning—A Death" is a masterpiece, capturing at once the new, sophisticated battlefield medicine of Vietnam and the ancient, ageless human misery and futility of all wars:

> You are dead just as finally
> As your mucosity dries on my lips
> In this morning sun.
> I have thumped and blown into your kind too often.
> I grow tired of kissing the dead.

Casey, a former military policeman, works exclusively with the truncated matter-of-fact speech rhythms that mirror the Vietnam grunts' favorite phrase: "There it is"—no further explanation offered. "School children walk by," he writes in "On Death":

> Some stare
> Some keep on walking
> Some adults stare too
> With handkerchiefs
> Over their nose
>   ***
> No jaw
> Intestines poured
> Out of the stomach
> The penis in the air
>   It won't matter then to me   but now
> I don't want in death to be a
> Public obscenity like this[.]

With the passage of time, Casey's poems seem less substantial than former medic Paquet's, but back then they were deemed good enough to earn him the Yale Younger Poets Award, and his collection *Obscenities* appeared almost simultaneously with *Winning Hearts and Minds.*

Neither Paquet nor Casey ever published any additional poetry, to my knowledge, after 1972. But for others in the volume, and for Vietnam-related poetry in general, *Winning Hearts and Minds* proved to be only the forerunner for a body of poetry that, 14 years later, is still growing. Many of the poets, like Paquet and Casey, surfaced briefly, then disappeared. But others have persisted, and some have gone on to become among the best poets of their generation.

Even before 1972 ended, D. C. Berry's *saigon cemetery* appeared from the University of Georgia Press. Another former medic, Berry offers a vision of the war in which "hope" (and almost everything else) appears in lower case:

> the boy's ma said may
> be he's one of the Lord's

> pretty flowers'll rise
> resurrection day —
>   "God woman ain't
> no dead bulb gonna rise this May
> never! God
>   pity you Martha!"

In many of Berry's poems, lines, pieces of lines and words are scattered across the page like dismembered body parts, mimicking that all-too-frequent reality of the war.

Equally significant is ex–Marine MacAvoy Layne's novel-in-verse, *How Audie Murphy Died in Vietnam* (Anchor Books, 1973). In 227 very short and often bleakly humorous poems, Layne traces the life of his fictional Audie Murphy from birth through childhood to enlistment in the Marines, then boot camp, a tour of duty in Vietnam — including capture by the North Vietnamese — and finally home again. Some of the poems are as short as "Guns":

> When the M-16 rifle had a stoppage,
> One could feel enemy eyes
> Climbing
> His
> Bones
> Like
> Ivy.

None is longer than a single page. Though few, if any, could stand up alone without the support of all the others, their cumulative effect is remarkable and convincing.

A more durable poet — indeed, one of the very best — is John Balaban. His first book-length collection, *After Our War* (University of Pittsburgh, 1974), deservedly won the Lamont Award from the Academy of American Poets.

Balaban is an anomaly: a soldier-poet who was not a soldier; indeed, he opposed the war and became a conscientious objector. But he chose to do his alternative service in Vietnam, first as a teacher of linguistics at the University of Can Tho, then as field representative for the Committee of Responsibility to Save War-Injured Children. Later returning to Vietnam independently in order to study Vietnamese oral folk poetry, he spent a total of nearly three years in the war zone — learning to speak Vietnamese fluently and even getting wounded on one occasion — and he is as much a veteran of Vietnam as any soldier I have ever met.

Because of his unique situation, however, Balaban brings to his poetry a perspective unlike any other. "A poet had better keep his mouth shut," he writes in "Saying Good-by to Mr. and Mrs. My, Saigon, 1972":

> unless he's found words to comfort and teach.
> Today, comfort and teaching themselves deceive
> and it takes cruelty to make any friends
> when it is a lie to speak, a lie to keep silent.

While Balaban's poems offer little comfort, they have much to teach. Years before Agent Orange was widely acknowledged for the silent killer it is—the deadly seed sown in Asia only to take root at home among those who thought they'd survived—Balaban wrote in "Along the Mekong":

> With a scientific turn of mind I can understand
> that malformations in lab mice may not occur in children
> but when, last week, I ushered hare-lipped, tusk-toothed
>   kids
> to surgery in Saigon, I wondered, what had they drunk
> that I have drunk.

And his "The Guard at the Binh Thuy Bridge" is a frightening exercise in quiet tension—the way it was; the war always a hair-trigger away, just waiting to happen:

> How still he stands as mists begin to move,
> as morning, curling, billows creep across
> his cooplike, concrete sentry perched mid-bridge
> over mid-muddy river.
>   * * *
> Anchored in red morning mist a narrow junk
> rocks its weight. A woman kneels on deck
> staring at lapping water. Wets her face.
> Idly the thick Rach Binh Thuy slides by.
> He aims. At her. Then drops his aim. Idly.

Balaban is particularly adept at contrasting the impact of the war on Vietnam with the indifference of those at home. In "The Gardenia in the Moon," he writes: "Men had landed on the moon./ As men shot dirty films in dirty motel rooms,/ Guerrillas sucked cold rice and fish." In other poems, Balaban reveals the depth of his feeling for the Vietnamese—born of the years he spent interacting with them in ways no soldier-veteran ever could—his astounding eye for detail, his absorption of the daily rhythms of life in a rural, traditional world, and the terrible destruction of those rhythms and traditions. In "Orpheus in the Upper World," he offers perhaps an explanation for the hundreds and even thousands of poems written by those who fought the war:

> For when his order had burst his head,
> like sillowy seeds of milkweed pod,
> he learned to pay much closer watch
> to all things, even small things,
> as if to discover his errors.

Not all the poems in *After Our War* deal with Vietnam. But if some of the non–Vietnam poems occasionally reveal the graduate student laboring to flex his intellectual muscle, they also reveal the poet's ability to transcend Vietnam and reach out to the wider world around him.

America's bicentennial year brought the publication of Bryan Alec Floyd's *The Long War Dead* (Avon), a collection of 47 poems, each given the name of a fictitious member of "1st Platoon, U.S.M.C." Floyd, a Vietnam-era Marine, did not actually serve in the war zone. But his poems are based on discussions with numerous Vietnam veterans, and they ripple with authority. "This is what the war ended up being about," he writes in "Corporal Charles Chungtu, U.S.M.C.":

> we would find a V.C. village,
> and if we could not capture it
> or clear it of Cong,
> we called for jets.
>   ***
> Then the village
> that was not a village any more
> was our village.

Floyd's poems have marvelous range, giving voice to those who supported the war and those who detested it, lashing out with equal vehemence at American generals and north Vietnamese diplomats, the anti-war movement and the failed war. He succeeds, like no other poet I know of, in offering the full breadth of feelings and emotions of those who fought the war.

Equally important was a new anthology, *Demilitarized Zones* (East River Anthology), co-edited by Jan Barry and myself. Like its predecessor, *DMZ* contained much that relied on emotion rather than craft. But it offered additional work by *WHAM* poets Barry, Cross, Krohn, Purcell and others, as well as new work by Balaban and Berry.

It also introduced a handful of good newcomers. Ex-infantry-man Steve Hassett contributes half-a-dozen poems, including his eerily ironic "Christmas," in which "The Hessian in his last letter home/ said in part/ 'they are all rebels here/ who will not stand to fight/ but each time fade before us/ as water into sand[.]'" Former Airman Horace Coleman writes of his "Saigon daughter" in "A Black Soldier Remembers":

> She does not offer me one of the
> silly hats she sells Americans and
> I have nothing she needs but
> the sad smile she already has.

In "Death of a Friend," ex-artilleryman Doug Rawlings writes, "his death/ begs me to follow/ pulls me toward him/ my hands grow weak/ and/ cannot break/ the string[.]" There are also excellent poems by Gerald McCarthy and Bruce Weigl, both of whom would later publish book-length collections of their own.

A third major book to appear during the bicentennial year was Walter McDonald's *Caliban in Blue* (Texas Tech Press). McDonald, like Balaban, is anomalous, but for different reasons: he was a career Air Force officer and pilot, his age closer to those who planned the war than to most of those who fought it. But his poems are wonderfully powerful, often intimately personal and sensitive. In "Faraway Places," he writes:

> This daughter watching ducks knows
> nothing of Vietnam,
> this pond her only Pacific,
> separation to her
> only the gulf between herself
> and ducks that others feed.
>   ***
>   Strange prospect
> to leave such gold, he thinks.
> There is no gold for him
> in Asia.
>   ***
>   Possession

turns on him like swimming ducks,
forcing his touch again.

She does not feel his claim
upon her gold
that swirls upon her face but cannot blink
her eyes
so full of ducks.

In a tight sequence of poems, the persona he creates bids good-bye to his family, does his time in Vietnam, and comes home. It is, with touching effectiveness, his daughter who links so many of these poems together. In "Rocket Attack," he first describes the death of a young Vietnamese girl, then cries out:

Daughter, oh God, my daughter
may she never
safe at home
Never hear the horrible
sucking sound a rocket makes when it

— and there the poem ends, as abruptly as consciousness at the moment of impact. Finally, home at last, "The Retired Pilot to Himself" wonders:

Bombs so long falling; after falling,
what release?

       O for tonight —

my child
with benediction
sidling heel and toe in graceful
rhapsody,
acceptance of herself.

In one particularly striking poem, "Interview with a Guy Named Fawkes, U.S. Army," he captures — as well as any young "grunt" could — the grinding frustrations of guerrilla war:

— —you tell them this— —
tell them shove it, they're
not here, tell them kiss
my rear when they piss about
women and kids in shacks
we fire on. damn.
they fire on us.
    ***

> what do they know back where
> not even in their granddam's days
> did any damn red rockets glare.

In addition, a number of very good non–Vietnam poems in *Caliban in Blue* attest to McDonald's great skill and expanding field of vision.

The following year brought McCarthy's solid collection, *War Story* (The Crossing Press). The first section of the book is a sequence of 22 untitled poems set mostly in the war zone, but as the book progresses, the poems become richer and more haunting as the full impact of the war slowly settles in upon the former Marine. In "The Sound of Guns," he writes:

> At the university in town
> tight-lipped men tell me the war in Vietnam is over,
> that my poems should deal with other things[.]
>   ***
> At nineteen I stood at night and watched
> an airfield mortared. A plane that was to take
> me home, burning; men running out of the flames.
>
> Seven winters have slipped away,
> the war still follows me.
> Never in anything have I found
> a way to throw off the dead.

It would be another two years before Weigl would publish his first book-length collection, *A Romance* (University of Pittsburgh). Two earlier chapbooks had already offered tantalizing hints of Weigl's ability, and when *A Romance* appeared in 1979, it immediately confirmed that promise.

Again, one finds the particular hallmark of the very best of the soldier-poets: scattered among the war-related poems are numerous excellent poems on other topics, suggesting an ability to transcend Vietnam. Indeed, of the 36 poems, only ten deal with the war. Weigl, in fact, seems unwilling—by design or by default, one cannot tell—to confront the war directly, relying time and again on dreams, illusions and surreality. "Sailing to Bien Hoa" is typical:

> In my dream of the hydroplane
> I'm sailing to Bien Hoa
> the shrapnel in my thighs
> like tiny glaciers.

> I remember a flower,
> a kite, a mannikin playing the guitar,
> a yellow fish eating a bird, a truck
> floating in urine, a rat carrying a banjo,
> a fool counting the cards, a monkey praying,
> a procession of whales, and far off
> two children eating rice,
> speaking French —
> I'm sure of the children,
> their damp flutes,
> the long line of their vowels.

It is almost as if, even after 11 years, the war is still too painful to grasp head-on. Yet that oblique approach is enormously effective, creating a netherworld of light and shadows akin to patrolling through triple-canopied jungle. In "Mines," he writes:

> Here is how you walk at night: slowly lift
> one leg, clear the sides with your arms, clear the back,
> front, put the leg down, like swimming.

And in "Monkey," a complicated five-part poem, he writes:

> I like a little unaccustomed mercy.
> Pulling the trigger is all we have.
> I hear a child.
>   ***
> I'm tired of the rice
> falling in slow motion[.]

Each one of these ten poems, scattered as they are among the others, is like stepping into a punji pit or triggering a tripwire.

Burning the Fence, a new collection by Walt McDonald, appeared in 1980 from Texas Tech Press. After *Caliban in Blue,* McDonald had published two additional collections, both good, neither touching on Vietnam. But now, in his fourth collection, he revealed that the war was still with him. In "The Winter Before the War," he talks of raking leaves in late autumn, the approach of winter, the first snow and ice-fishing, concluding:

> The fireplace
> after dark
> was where we thawed.
> Chocolate steamed
> in mugs we wrapped
> our hands around.

> Our children slept.
> The news came on.
> We watched
> each other's eyes.

Only in "Al Croom," in fact, does he write of Vietnam directly, and the word "Vietnam" appears nowhere in the collection. But the war is there, nevertheless, like a dark and brooding presence.

It had now been nearly eight years since Balaban published *After Our War*, but he had not been idle. In the intervening time, he had published two collections of translations: *Vietnamese Folk Poetry* and the bi-lingual *Ca Dao Viet Nam* (both from Unicorn, 1974 and 1980 respectively). And in 1982, his *Blue Mountain* (also from Unicorn) ably demonstrated the growth of his own poetry over the years. Here are poems ranging from the American West to the southern Appalachians, from Pennsylvania to Romania, along with eloquent elegies to friends and family members.

Still, lingering memories of Vietnam persist. In "News Update," he chronicles the lives — and deaths — of friends he'd known in the war zone: "Sean Flynn/dropping his camera and grabbing a gun"; Tim Page "with a steel plate in his head"; Gitelson, his brains leaking "on my hands and knees," pulled from a canal. "And here I am, ten years later," he muses:

> written up in the local small town press
> for popping a loud-mouth punk in the choppers.
> Oh, big sighs. Windy sighs. And ghostly laughter.

In "For Mrs. Cam, Whose Name Means 'Printed Silk,'" he reflects on the dislocation of the refugee boat people:

> The wide Pacific flares in sunset.
> Somewhere over there was once your home.
> You study the things which start from scratch.

And in "After Our War," he writes:

> After our war, the dismembered bits
> — all those pierced eyes, ear slivers, jaw splinters,
> gouged lips, odd tibias, skin flaps, and toes —
> came squinting, wobbling, jabbering back.

After observing wryly that "all things naturally return to their source," he wonders, "After our war, how will love speak?"

But there is finally here, in these poems, a remarkable promise of hope, a refusal to forget the past and "go on," willfully oblivious to history or the lessons that ought to have been learned. In "In Celebration of Spring," he insists:

> Swear by the locust, by dragonflies on ferns,
> by the minnow's flash, the tremble of a breast,
> by the new earth spongy under our feet:
> that as we grow old, we will not grow evil,
> that although our garden seeps with sewage,
> and our elders think it's up for auction — swear
> by this dazzle that does not wish to leave us —
> that we will be keepers of a garden, nonetheless.

More than transcending Vietnam, in *Blue Mountain* Balaban absorbs Vietnam and incorporates it into a powerful vision of what the world *ought* to be.

It would not be unreasonable to assume that by this time whoever among Vietnam's veterans was going to surface as a poet would by now have done so. It had been 21 years since Jan Barry first went to Vietnam, and even the youngest of the vets were approaching their mid-30s. But the appearance in 1984 of D. F. Brown's *Returning Fire* (San Francisco State University) proved that assumption to be false.

Former medic Brown is particularly interesting, having remained in the army from 1968 to 1977, and one can only wonder why he stayed in and why he got out. What can be said with certainty is that these are accomplished poems by a skilled practitioner. All of them deal with Vietnam and its aftermath. "I can tell true stories/of the jungle," he writes in "When I Am 19 I Was a Medic":

> I sleep strapped to a .45,
> bleached into my fear.
> I do this under the biggest tree,
> some nights I dig
> in saying my wife's name
> over and over.
>   ***
>   I never mention
> the fun, our sense of humor
> embarrasses me. Something
> warped it out of place
> and bent I drag it along —
> keep track of time spent,
> measure what I think we have left.

In "Eating the Forest," he speaks of "soldiers/ trained to sleep/ where the moon sinks/ and bring the darkness home[.]" In "Still Later There Are War Stories," he warns: "We grow old counting the year/ in days, . . . The jungle/ loaded, nobody/ comes away in one piece." And in "Coming Home," he notices:

> Someone has stacked his books,
> Records, souvenirs, pretending
> This will always be light
> And zoned residential[.]

The shortest poem in the book is "L'Eclatante Victoire de Khe Sanh":

> The main thing
> to remember
> is the jungle
> has retaken the trenches—
>
> think it forgiven
> look on it healed
> as a scar.

The longest poem, from which the book's title is taken, runs over three pages. In between are some of the best poems to come out of the war. Whether Brown will eventually expand his reach to include other subjects and themes remains to be seen, but *Returning Fire* is a strong beginning.

Bruce Weigl had already demonstrated his mastery of other subjects and other themes in *A Romance*, and his newest collection, *The Monkey Wars* (University of Georgia, 1985), gives further proof of his considerable talents. Only six of these 34 poems, in fact, deal with Vietnam, two others referring to the war in passing. Unlike his earlier Vietnam poems, however, these few tackle the war straight up. Absent are the dreams and illusions, the surreality. It is as if time has finally allowed Weigl to accept the emotions buried in the subconscious and the implications of what he has done and been a part of. In the tellingly brutal and straightforward poem "Burning Shit at An Khe," he describes in painful detail the repulsive task of cleaning makeshift outhouses:

> I tried to light a match
>   It died
> And it all came down on me, the stink
>   And the heat and the worthlessness

Until I slipped and climbed
   Out of that hole and ran
Past the olive drab
   Tents and trucks and clothes and everything
Green as far from the shit
   As the fading light allowed.
Only now I can't fly.
   I lie down in it
And finger paint the words of who I am
   Across my chest
Until I'm covered and there's only one smell,
   One word.

Even more chilling is "Song of Napalm," in which he tries to appreciate the wonder of horses in a pasture after a storm:

Still I close my eyes and see the girl
Running from her village, napalm
Stuck to her dress like jelly,
Her hands reaching for the no one
Who waits in waves of heat before her.
   ***
So I can keep on living,
So I can stay here beside you,
I try to imagine she runs down the road and wings
Beat inside her until she rises
Above the stinking jungle and her pain
Eases, and your pain, and mine.

But the poem continues, "the lie swings back again," and finally:

...she is burned behind my eyes
And not your good love and not the rain-swept air
And not the jungle green
Pasture unfolding before us can deny it.

Perhaps because he has come to terms with the worst, he can also now remember with a certain amusement "The Girl at the Chu Lai Laundry," who wouldn't give him his uniforms because they weren't finished:

Who would've thought the world stops
Turning in the war, the tropical heat like hate
And your platoon moves out without you,
Your wet clothes piled
At the feet of the girl at the laundry,
Beautiful with her facts.

|

These are wonderful poems, made more so by their juxtaposition with touchingly beautiful non-war poems like "Snowy Egret" and "Small Song for Andrew." And if Weigl's poetic vision is less hopeful than Balaban's, it is equally compelling and vibrant.

Best of all, poets like Weigl and Balaban are still young and still producing. One hopes for the same from Brown, McCarthy and others. A poem of McDonald's appeared recently in *The Atlantic*. And other poets may yet emerge. Vietnam veteran Yusef Komunyakaa has published excellent poems in recent years in magazines and anthologies, and a collection of his, *I Apologize for the Eyes in My Head*, is forthcoming from Wesleyan University Press. Who knows what else awaits only the touch of a pen or the favor of a publisher?

There remains, for now, only speculation as to why Vietnam has produced such an impressive body of poems (not to mention short stories, novels and personal narratives) — especially considering the relative paucity of poems arising from other modern American wars. Korea produced almost nothing at all. From World War II, one can think of only a handful of poems like James Dickey's "The Firebombing," Randall Jarrell's "The Death of the Ball Turret Gunner," and sections of Thomas McGrath's *Letter to an Imaginary Friend*. The contrast is even more remarkable when one considers how very few members of the Vietnam Generation ever actually served in Vietnam in any capacity at all. Where then do these poems come from?

Surely it has to do with the peculiar nature of the war itself. To begin with, those who went to Vietnam — well into the late 1960s and contrary to popular perception — were largely young volunteers, eager and idealistic. The average age of American soldiers in Vietnam was 19 ½ (in World War II, it had been 26). They had grown up in the shadow of their fathers' generation, the men who had fought "the good war" from 1941 to 1945. Most had been in grade school or junior high school when John F. Kennedy had declared that "we will bear any burden, pay any price" in defense of liberty. They were young enough to have no worldly experience whatsoever, they had absorbed the values of their society wholesale, and they had no earthly reason prior to their arrival in Vietnam to doubt either their government or the society that willingly acquiesced in their going.

All of that was about to change forever. Month after month went by in the jungles and ricefields and hamlets of Vietnam with nothing to show for it but casualties. Men fought and died for nameless hills, only to walk away from them when the battle was over. Men taught to believe that American soldiers handed out candy to kids found themselves killing and being killed by those very kids. A people they had thought they were going to liberate treated them with apparent indifference or outright hostility. Progress was measured in grisly official body counts, and any dead Vietnamese was a Viet Cong. Torture, assault and battery, malicious destruction, murder and mayhem — the very things young Americans had always been taught only the enemy did — were widespread and tacitly or openly sanctioned. Worst of all, as time passed, it became obvious even to the most naive 18-year-old that the war was going nowhere.

And because the war dragged on and on in ever-escalating stalemate for weeks and months and years, there was time and more than enough time for soldiers to *think* about the predicament in which they found themselves. Who in the hell was fighting whom? Why?! And for what? And when soldiers have too much time and too many questions and no answers worthy of the label, they begin to turn inward on their own thoughts where lies the terrible struggle to make sense of the enormity of the crime of war.

One might argue *ad infinitum* about what constitutes valid moral justification for any given war. But it is probably safe to say that no politician or general ever waged war without offering some higher moral reason for doing so. Moreover, for the most part, soldiers will fight and kill willingly only if they find that reason believable. Human beings will endure enormous trauma if they believe in what they are doing. But the explanations given by those who'd sent the soldiers to fight in Vietnam became ever more surreal and absurd until they were revealed for what they were: nothing but empty words, bereft of reason or any semblance of higher moral authority.

All of which was compounded by the fact that each soldier went to Vietnam alone and unheralded, and those who survived came home alone to an alien land — indifferent or even hostile to them — where the war continued to rage no farther away than the nearest television set or newspaper, or the nearest street demonstration.

Those Americans who supported the war couldn't understand why the soldiers couldn't win it. Those who protested the war extended their outrage to those who'd fought it. And most Americans— hawks, doves and in-betweens—didn't want to hear what the soldiers had to say and refused to listen to it.

In short, those who had been asked and ordered to pull the trigger were left alone to carry the weight of the entire disaster that was America's war in Indochina. The American people turned their backs on the war long before it ended. Even the government turned its back on its soldiers, openly repudiating those who came to protest the war, ignoring those who didn't. Veterans Administration benefits were a paltry disgrace—and even the little that was offered had to be fought for tooth and nail. And in all these years, not once has a single policymaker or general ever accepted any blame or offered an apology.

Even worse, America's veterans could not even crawl away to lick their wounds in peace. Without even the illusion of a satisfactory resolution, the war ground on for years after most veterans had come home, and the fall of Saigon has been followed by one reminder after another: the boat people, the amnesty issue, Agent Orange, delayed stress, the occupation of Cambodia, the bombing of the Marine barracks in Beirut, the mining of Nicaragua's harbors. And the initial rejection of Vietnam veterans, and the long silence of the seventies which followed (during which time Vietnam veterans were routinely stereotyped as drug-crazed, emotionally unbalanced misfits), have only given way to Rambo, Chuck Norris and the sorry spectacle of America's Vietnam veterans driven to build monuments to themselves and throw parades in their own honor.

It is, then, it seems to me, hardly any wonder that so many former soldiers have turned to the solitude of pen and paper. Under such conditions as these, there have been more than enough reason and plenty of time for once-idealistic youngsters to consider long and hard the war they fought, the government and the society that sent them to fight it, and the values they had once believed in. While many of these writers might be loathe to call themselves anti-war poets, few if any have anything good to say about their experience in Vietnam.

In 1963, John Kennedy said in a speech at Amherst College, "When power corrupts, poetry cleanses." Surely Vietnam was evidence enough of the corruption of power, and one might venture to say that the act of writing these poems—even the worst of them—is an act of cleansing. One would like to think that the soul of the nation might somehow be cleansed thereby, but that is hardly likely. More realistically, one hopes that in writing these poems, the poets might at least have begun to cleanse their own souls of the torment that was and is Vietnam. Surely, in the process of trying, the best of them have added immeasurably to the body and soul of American poetry.

LOS NORTEAMERICANOS
Y CENTROAMÉRICA

Quetzalina Yali is a four-year-old bundle of brown curls and laughter. Undaunted by the small fact that I cannot understand a word she is saying, she chatters away in Spanish, the language brought to her country 400 years ago by the conquistadors. Pulling small pieces of cotton from a pinata made up to look like a rabbit, she pretends to fashion a beard and moustache for herself, but can't get the cotton to stay in place. I show her how to lick the cotton lightly, moistening it, so that it will stick wherever she wants it. Delighted with this new discovery, she plants a wad of cotton on the tip of my nose, then makes a goatee for herself.

We are on our way to San Jose de los Remates, a village of several thousand people in the mountains about 90 kilometers northeast of Managua, Nicaragua. Quetzalina's father, Flavio Galo, 28, is driving the Toyota Land Cruiser. Beside him are his wife, Carmen, 26, and Reverend David Funkhouser, 41, an Episcopal minister who is director of the Central America Organizing Project [CAOP], a community action group working out of West Philadelphia, Pennsylvania. David, a close friend of the Galos, has been to Nicaragua eight times since the 1979 revolution, and it is he who has arranged our trip. With Quetzalina and me in back is Peter Morgan, 30, a freelance photographer.

The two-lane macadam road passes by a large Cuban-built sugar refinery, then skirts the edge of a brand-new dam and reservoir guarded by Nicaraguan soldiers against potential terrorist attack by the U.S.-backed "Contras," whom many Nicaraguans call "mer-

cenaries." At the village of Teustepe, we leave the paved road and
the flat plain around Managua, and head up into the mountains on
a rough one-lane dirt track heavily rutted by erosion. Five times our
vehicle must ford streams because there are no bridges, and our
progress is further impeded by regular encounters with small herds
of cattle plodding along the road, each herd tended by a man or boy
on horseback.

The bumpy, twisting dirt road between Teustepe and San Jose
was built by the people of this region in 1974 with nothing more
sophisticated than picks and shovels, ox-carts and mules. Prior to
that time, a road connecting San Jose to the capital city and the
government of Nicaragua simply did not exist. Once a day now, in
the early morning, a bus leaves San Jose for the four-hour drive to
Managua, returning late in the afternoon.

Peter offers a stick of gum to Quetzalina. Without hesitating, she
takes the gum, tears it in half and thrusts a piece over the front seat
into her mother's mouth. Carmen Galo was raised in San Jose.
During the revolution, she was a member of the "retroguard,"
building barricades, gathering information, and carrying intelligence and supplies to the Sandinista fighters. After "the
triumph of the revolution," as she calls it, she became a
Brigadista—a volunteer member of the Literacy Crusade. While
working in the countryside, she met Flavio, who was then serving
two years in the regular army. They were married in 1980, and
Quetzalina arrived two years later.

Soon after we turn onto the dirt road, Quetzalina—whose name
means "Queen of Birds"—curls up in my lap and falls asleep, im-
pervious to the violent jostling we are being subjected to by the
crude road surface. Her middle name, Yali, is the name of a town
near which a close friend of Flavio and Carmen was killed fighting
the Contras. One of Flavio's brothers was also killed by Contras
while harvesting coffee in 1981. Neither Flavio nor Carmen has any
doubts about the path their country has set itself upon: they feel
they are building a future for their daughter.

Flavio's mother, Norma Galo, still lives in the Parish of San
Pablo in Nicarao, a working-class barrio of Managua where Flavio
and his brothers grew up. In 1966, when Flavio was 8, Norma and
some other concerned adults organized a Base Christian Community with the help of the parish priest and a Maryknoll nun from

the United States (one of four American women who would be
raped and murdered by members of the Salvadoran army 14 years
later). Norma and the others wanted to do something to combat illiteracy, drug addiction among young people, and the general
sense of hopelessness that pervaded the barrio.

"At first, the young people didn't want anything to do with Chris-
tianity," Norma told our group. "'Somoza and the bishops are the
same thing,' they said. But we developed a program that finally got
them interested." Listening to the young people's suggestions, they
devised new rules for worship to make the mass less distant and
alien: no cassocks for the priest, no kneeling during communion,
face-to-face confession, and the mass said in Spanish rather than
Latin. Soon, the active members of the parish, adults and young
people alike, were involved in teaching others to read and write,
and in attempting to bring minimal public health standards to the
barrio.

By 1969, the parish had developed a popular peasant mass that
included songs by the renowned Nicaraguan priest and poet
Ernesto Cardinal (now Minister of Culture in the Sandinista
government). Much of the mass was critical of the U.S.-backed
Somoza dictatorship and the church hierarchy, Norma explained,
taking the side of the peasants and the poor. "We had always been
taught that poverty and suffering were virtues that would be re-
warded in heaven," said Norma, "but we began to understand that
the Kingdom of God must begin here on earth."

Taking advantage of their new-found literacy, for the first time
the parishioners began to read the Bible for themselves. "We
learned from the Bible that what God wants most is justice," said
Norma. "It was not possible to separate religious consciousness
from political consciousness. We began to study our own history.
We began to see that Somoza and his generals had gotten rich from
the suffering of our people, and that the exploitation of the poor
went back all the way to colonial times. And we learned that the
young people had been right all along: the church hierarchy has
always acted in support of the status quo, reinforcing the system
as it is."

Thus, it came as no surprise, Norma continued, when the
church hierarchy and the Somoza regime together cracked down
on the Base Christian Communities. The church forbade the peasant mass, and Somoza banned all "political activities," including

efforts to improve literacy and public health. Still, the peasant mass was said in San Pablo, and the political organizing continued. "At times, I wondered if I was crazy to take such risks," Norma said, "but we couldn't do anything else. The repression was intolerable. We had to take risks because Jesus took risks."

In such an atmosphere, Flavio grew up. By this time, Norma explained, the Sandinista National Liberation Front [FSLN] was actively fighting Somoza's hated National Guard in the mountains. "We began to see that they were the only real possibility for change," she said. "They were fighting for justice, and so were we Christians." In 1972, Flavio, at 14 already an accomplished guitarist, helped to found GRADAS, the first cultural-political organization of the FSLN. He was joined by the singer and composer Carlos Mejia Godoy and the young poet Rosario Murillo, who would later marry Daniel Ortega, now president of Nicaragua.

Together the members of GRADAS would sing their songs in parks and factories, on streetcorners and vacant lots, coupling their overt activities with covert political organizing. In 1974, Flavio was arrested and imprisoned by Somoza. In 1976, Godoy and Murillo went into foreign exile. Then in 1978, Flavio was arrested again, this time for organizing a strike of public workers. He was tortured continuously for 15 days in a dark one-person cubicle in La Chiquita Prison. After his release, he finally took up arms, eventually becoming the leader of a 250-person guerrilla unit operating in and around Managua.

By this time, the resistance movement had erupted into mass insurrection, and Somoza's days were numbered. "Your president claims that Cuba and the Soviet Union helped us," Norma scoffed, "but that is not true. They gave us nothing. We made our own weapons." Norma made Molotov Cocktails. Flavio's 10-year-old brother made contact mines. "Our fighters attacked the National Guard with these homemade weapons," she explained, "then they would capture the M-16s of the Guardsmen. Every time I was brought more captured weapons to hide, I would get down on my knees and thank God.

"I am a Catholic and a Christian," Norma said emphatically, "and I don't care what your president says — or the Pope, either. The revolution is an affirmation of our Christian faith because we are able to do things now that we were never able to do before. We didn't learn that from Marx and Lenin. We learned it from the Bible. The church is us. We have to fight for a better world. We don't want a new church. We want our own church to be reborn. All we ask is that the bishops, for the first time in history, walk by the side of the poor."

Not everyone, of course, perceives the Sandinista revolution as a Christian endeavor. During last spring's heated debate over the $100 million Contra aid bill—which finally passed the House of Representatives by the slimmest of margins only weeks before our July 14, 1986, departure—Ronald Reagan said that the Sandinistas ought to be pushed "right back to Havana where they belong." The archbishops of Boston and New York have castigated the Nicaraguan government for its "attempts to violate the religious conscience of Nicaraguans." And a poster from the National Democratic Front [FDN], the largest of the U.S.-backed counterrevolutionary groups waging war against the Sandinistas, contains a portrait of a smiling Jesus, together with the words: "Christ is our liberator."

In fact, were one to take at face value the pronouncements of those who oppose the Sandinista government, one could only conclude that Nicaragua today is little more than a Third World version of the Soviet Union. Having lived through a combat tour as a Marine volunteer in Vietnam, however, I have long since grown wary of bureaucrats and politicians who would have me believe that the world, or any part thereof, can be neatly divided into "freedom fighters" and "terrorists"—the freedom fighters, of course, always being on our side. After all, it is my tax dollars the Contras are spending, and my own child may one day be asked or even ordered to fight in Nicaragua. And so I made up my mind to see Nicaragua for myself.

That, as it turns out, is surprisingly easy to do—at least for now. One need only hook up with any number of U.S.-based organizations like David Funkhouser's CAOP, plunk your money down (about $1200 for a two-week trip), get on the airplane and go. For our trip, travel arrangements were made by a commercial travel agency in New York City in much the same manner as any tourist trip to England or the Bahamas. The Nicaraguan government issues tourist visas at the airport in Managua, and for now the U.S. government has been unable or politically unwilling to stop what has become a constant flow of U.S. citizens into Nicaragua, though it must surely be a major irritant for the Reagan administration.

Our two-week trip did not begin in Nicaragua, however, but rather in Honduras where, since the early 1980s, the U.S. has maintained a military presence fluctuating between 1,100 and over 5,000 soldiers. For three days, in the capital city of Tegucigalpa, at the U.S. base at Palmerola, and in the nearby town of Comayagua, we met with everyone from parish priests to peasant labor leaders, U.S. military personnel to opposition newspaper editors.

At the U.S. embassy in Tegucigalpa, we were told that the 15 U.S. Marine guards assigned to the embassy are responsible only for internal security. External security, including the policy that no photographs may be taken of or near the embassy grounds, is entirely the responsibility of the Hondurans.

Only moments later, as we drove away from the embassy, I made the mistake of absent-mindedly taking my camera from its pouch. Immediately, whistles began to blow all over the street, and we were flagged down by a Honduran security officer toting a shotgun. He thought I'd taken a picture and wanted to confiscate my camera. Two more armed officers arrived as I got out of the van, then two more. It was a tense situation. I was surrounded by five men armed with pistols, shotguns and M-16s, but I refused to hand over the camera.

Finally, the Hondurans insisted that I accompany them back to the embassy. They took me straight to the U.S. Marine guard inside the front door, a junior enlisted man. "I give you my word as an ex–Marine," I told the sentry, lifting my sleeve to reveal my USMC tattoo, "I did not take any photographs." With a single affirmative nod, the young corporal settled the matter like Solomon sitting in judgment, instantly countermanding the Honduran security officers supposedly responsible for external security.

At the embassy, we were told that Palmerola is a Honduran air force base, and that the approximately 1,000 U.S. military personnel stationed there are only "tenants." With its tin and plywood barracks, sandbagged bunkers and rolls of coiled concertina wire, Palmerola, located 60 kilometers northeast of Tegucigalpa, looks very much like a typical U.S. battalion base camp in the earlier stages of the Vietnam war—and indeed, it turns out that Palmerola was built by the U.S. "for Honduras" with U.S. funds.

"We have no contact whatsoever with the Contras," a regular U.S. army lieutenant colonel stationed at Palmerola told us. "Furthermore, we are not allowed to train Honduran troops. We only engage in joint exercises with the Hondurans. We learn from each other." He went on to describe for us the various activities of U.S. personnel: medical and civic action programs, road-building and other construction projects, signal intelligence. What he described sounded curiously like the strategy in Vietnam that was variously called "Rural Pacification," "Revolutionary Development," and "Winning Hearts and Minds," though he called it "low-intensity warfare." Who this low-intensity warfare is directed against is hard to determine since the only guerrilla forces currently operating in Honduras are the U.S.-supported Nicaraguan Contras.

Later, a major in the Kansas National Guard assigned to Palmerola for 30 days explained enthusiastically that Honduras is a perfect place to train U.S. reserve forces "under realistic conditions." When I expressed my concern about deploying so many U.S. troops in an area of such international tension, the major replied that it may well be an attempt by the Reagan administration to create its own "Gulf of Tonkin Incident." The analogy was the major's, not mine.

Dr. Jorge Arturo Reina is a leading politician in the progressive faction of the Honduran Liberal Party. He has presidential aspirations. "Because every Central American dictator has always called himself democratic," he told us, "people don't really know what democracy is. Democracy doesn't mean voting one day and dying of hunger the next. Democracy doesn't mean voting one day and losing your job the next. Democracy means voting one day so that your life will be better the next.

"This is not and never has been the case in Honduras," he continued. "Seventy-eight percent of our children are malnourished. Functional illiteracy is higher than 62 percent. The unemployment rate is 34 percent, with another 40 percent underemployed. The majority of our people live and die without ever turning on an electric light or using indoor plumbing or seeing a doctor or dentist or teacher. We don't want a revolution like Nicaragua or a war like El Salvador, but our problems must be addressed.

"U.S. aid to Honduras is a mirage," he insisted. "You saw the airport in Tegucigalpa. It is totally inadequate. The U.S. has built nine new airports in Honduras, but none of them is for the Hondurans. The U.S. says it is building roads for us, but the roads only connect one military base to another. There is no U.S. policy for Honduras except to use Honduras as a base of operations to achieve U.S. aims in Nicaragua and El Salvador, while the problems of Honduras only continue to get worse.

"Mr. Reagan's policy is like an elephant in a china closet chasing a rat. It creates greater problems than those it tries to resolve. Aid to the Contras will not defeat the Sandinistas, but only radicalize them. And now the Contras have more money than we do! Their presence in our country has created 12,000 internal Honduran refugees who have been forced to flee Contra-held territory in Honduras. Mr. Reagan's policy is leading Honduras closer and closer to war. God blinds those who do not love."

The Honduran political headquarters of the Nicaraguan Contra group FDN is located in a comfortable villa on the outskirts of Tegucigalpa. There, we met with Francisco Arana, director of central communications, and four of the FDN's 18 regional field commanders. Most of the talking was done by Arana, a huge man who is a former banker, and Commandante Fernando, a former theological student who looked to be in his late 20s or early 30s. Two of the commandantes said nothing at all during the interview, but only sat motionless and glaring; it seemed to me that they did not like us very much.

"We wanted democracy and freedom," said Arana, "but the Sandinistas betrayed us."

I asked if it was true that the Contras are really the remnants of Somoza's old National Guard. "We don't refuse anyone just because he was once a National Guardsman or a Sandinista," said Commandante Fernando, a member of the fundamentalist United Pentacostal Mission. "Those who have National Guard connections fight now for love of God and the liberation of Nicaragua. The FDN represents the true democratic aspirations of the Nicaraguan people, but the Sandinista propaganda machine has painted the opposite picture."

What about alleged atrocities committed by the Contras against Honduran civilians, I asked. "That isn't possible," Arana replied.

"All of the fighting is taking place inside Nicaragua. There are no permanent Contra bases in Honduras. Honduran communists are committing these atrocities, and the FDN gets the blame. Believe me, the Sandinistas are financing all of the Honduran groups you've been talking with while you've been here."

David then asked about Contra terrorist attacks within Nicaragua, citing the July 4, 1986, destruction of a civilian truck by a contact mine that killed 34 people, mostly women and children. "I see you are already one of the convinced," Arana replied with a shrug.

"You are a victim of propaganda," added Commandante Fernando. "The civilian dead are killed by the Sandinistas, not the FDN, but the Sandinistas lie. The Sandinistas dress up like the FDN, then commit these atrocities themselves."

What about the U.S. Government Accounting Office report indicating that much of the aid already sent to the Contras has been siphoned off without ever reaching the field, I asked. "That is Sandinista disinformation," Arana replied.

"You mean the GAO compiled its report from information received from the Sandinistas?" I asked incredulously.

"Our leaders are always with us," Commandante Fernando replied vehemently. "Even without material aid, God's love and our love for Nicaragua keeps us going forward. We and the people of Nicaragua hope for the support of the government and the people of the United States. To compare Somoza with the Sandinistas, Somoza would be an angel. The Sandinistas are Marxists, and Marxists are atheists. The Sandinistas are enemies of God. With God and patriotism, we will defeat communism and liberate Nicaragua, Central America, and the United States."

As we left the FDN villa with its beautiful rose bushes and manicured lawn, I happened to glance up at the hill behind the FDN compound. Perched precariously atop the hill and on its steep slopes were several dozen tin and cardboard squatters shacks belonging to the poor of Honduras.

Roberto Flores Bermudez is Director of Foreign Policy Affairs for the Honduran Foreign Ministry. U.S. military activities in Honduras are beneficial, he explained, because they provide the Honduran army with equipment and training which will better enable Honduras to defend its territory and sovereignty—this despite the fact that U.S. officials at both the embassy and Palmerola told us explicitly that U.S. personnel are forbidden to train Honduran troops.

"Isn't it true," I asked, "that the Hondurans' traditional enemy is El Salvador?" (As recently as 1969, Honduras and El Salvador fought a brief but bloody war.) "How do you feel about the tremendous build-up of the Salvadoran army by the Reagan administration?"

"The internal situation in El Salvador requires it," he replied tersely.

"Doesn't the U.S. military presence in Honduras violate the Honduran constitution?" I asked.

"The U.S. presence is only temporary," he replied, echoing the assertions of U.S. officials.

"But we've been here for four years already. What would you call a permanent presence?"

"I wouldn't call Palmerola 'permanent,'" Bermudez responded. "It's only made of wood and tin."

"You mean, if it were made of concrete and steel, it would be permanent," I replied, "but since it's only wood and tin, it's temporary?"

Bermudez paused, smiling awkwardly: "Yes." As we left, I shook his hand and wished him and his country luck. "Thank you," he said quietly, "I think we will need it."

Given that U.S. embassy personnel in Honduras have told us that the Sandinistas wish to export communism and subversion to Honduras, it seems odd that Tan Sahsa, the Honduran airline, still maintains regular flights between Tegucigalpa and Managua. The young man who sat next to me is a medical doctor from Mexico. This was his third trip to Nicaragua since 1981, and he would be staying to work as a general practitioner for several months. "Why is Mr. Reagan so full of hate for these people?" he asked me. As the airplane touched down at Sandino Airport, he quietly said to himself, "Nicaragua libre."

The scene inside the airport was one of quiet pandemonium. It was two days before the July 19 seventh anniversary of the 1979 revolution, and the terminal was packed with incoming arrivals: Canadians, Swedes, Finns, French, Germans, Swiss, Israelis and Americans—whom Latin Americans call *Norteamericanos*. ("We live in America, too," I was told by Maria Antonia de Alvarado of the Honduran Federation of Women's Associations.) Because of the influx of people for the anniversary, security was especially tight, and our progress through customs was not helped by the grinding bureaucracy the Sandinistas have created. Every "t" had to be crossed, every "i" dotted on the visa applications. Bags had to be inspected. Names had to be checked and re-checked. But at last we cleared customs and headed into Managua.

The billboards in Nicaragua are not what I'd expected. Yes, there are the obligatory signs extolling the virtues of patriotism, the revolution and the Sandinistas. But there are also billboards urging people to support one or another of the various opposition parties, along with advertisements for Pepsi and Coca-Cola, Ciba-Geigy products, local restaurants and discotheques. Political graffiti of every stripe is everywhere, and there is even a McDonald's where one can buy a Big Mac and fried plantain cut to look like French fried potatoes.

Downtown Managua, however, is an eerie place. The capital was devastated by an earthquake in 1972, and the heart of the city was never rebuilt. Only the towering Bank of America building survived the quake, and now it looms up alone and forlorn amid overgrown vacant lots and the few remaining empty shells of other buildings, many inhabited by poor squatters. After the earthquake, the Somoza dictatorship received millions of dollars in international relief assistance. Instead of rebuilding the city, Somoza pocketed most of those funds.

Meals, we learned quickly, are always an adventure. On any given day, some restaurants haven't enough food to remain open. Others can offer only three or four entrees. In one restaurant, we were told that there was no fish or beef, but we could have chicken or pork. We ordered chicken. A half-hour later, we were told that there was no more chicken, but some fresh fish had just arrived. Food shortages are chronic, and tracking down one's favorite beverage—be it beer, orange soda or Coke—can be a haphazard and frustrating affair.

On July 19, well before dawn, we joined a bus caravan from Managua to the northern city of Esteli for the commemoration of the seventh anniversary. Every intersection along the 150 kilometer route, every bridge and culvert was guarded by soldiers, and as the sun rose, I could see other soldiers patrolling the high ground above the road. Clearly, great effort had been taken to see that the Contras would not disrupt the ceremony. As we neared Esteli, two Soviet-built helicopter gunships darted low among the hills.

Later that night, I was having a beer at the hotel bar in Pochomil when a middle-aged Nicaraguan approached me. "Thank you for coming to Nicaragua," he said in English. "I love the U.S. I love the North American people. We don't want war. We want to be friends." His name, he told me, is Santos, and he explained that he left Nicaragua in the early 1960s to escape Somoza's repression. He has lived in San Francisco for 23 years, and since the revolution, has worked as a Tur-Nica representative in the U.S. (Tur-Nica is the Nicaraguan state tourist agency.) As we talked further, we were joined by his friend, Ricardo. Their families have known each other since before Santos left Nicaragua.

"Are you a Sandinista, too?" I asked Ricardo, who manages a gas station.

"No!" he replied emphatically. "The Sandinistas have sold Nicaragua to the Cubans and the Russians. Things were better under Somoza. You could get anything then. Now everyone lives like shit."

"And you two guys are friends?" I asked Santos.

"Oh, sure!" Santos replied with a grin. "I don't agree with him, but he has his point of view, and it's important for you to hear it. In the United States, Reagan says that Nicaragua is totalitarian, but listen to Ricardo. He tells you what he thinks. Is that totalitarian? People should come to Nicaragua and see for themselves."

Sergio Murillo is a tractor driver on a private coffee farm in Carazo, a region between the Pacific coast and Managua. He earns 750 cordobas (about $.63) for an 8-hour shift, he told us during an impromptu interview amid rows of coffee plants, but if he wants to, he can work up to 12 shifts per week with double-time on Sunday. Wages are set by the state. The owner of the hacienda spends most of his time in Miami, Sergio told us, but after the revolution he gave each worker a small piece of land for a family plot. Sergio built his own house on his plot, where he lives with his wife and two children.

Sergio belongs to the Sandinista Workers Confederation, a union which grew out of the revolution. He likes the union because it gives the workers clout with their employers, and because the union commissary offers clothing and other goods at reduced prices. "Our biggest problem is food distribution and rationing," he said. "Each person receives only four pounds of rice per month, which is not enough. Because of the war in the north"—the Contra war—"many good farming areas can't be cultivated, and our fighters must have first priority on the food that's available. If there were a more peaceful dialogue between Nicaragua and the United States, everyone would benefit. Surely, there are hungry people in your country, too. This war is foolish."

Niquinohomo, just up the road from the coffee farm, is the town in which Augusto Cezar Sandino was born and lived. Sandino, namesake of the Sandinistas, is the greatest of all Nicaraguan heroes. His modest house is now a museum, but we arrived on Sunday afternoon, the house was locked, and no one seemed to know who had the key, so we had to settle for a stroll through the courtyard.

Being an ex–Marine, I have a healthy respect for this carpenter's son who managed to fight the U.S. Marine Corps to a draw. The Marines have a long history of involvement in Nicaragua, dating back almost to the turn of the century, including maintaining a permanent garrison there from 1912 to 1926 and again from 1927 to 1934. During those years, the Marines ruled Nicaragua as an occupied country, acting to protect the interests of U.S. businesses. It is an aspect of U.S. history that most Nicaraguans know more about than do most Americans. (To this day, the Nicaraguan version of the "bogeyman" is a *Yanqui* Marine.)

Beginning in 1927, Sandino waged a guerrilla war against the Marines that ended seven years later only when the United States agreed to withdraw the Marines. In their place, however, the U.S. government created, trained and equipped the Nicaraguan National Guard, which was placed under the command of a man named Anastasio Somoza Garcia.

Meanwhile, after the departure of the Marines, Sandino emerged from the hills and re-entered Nicaragua's political mainstream. Then one night in 1934, members of the National Guard kidnapped Sandino, took him out to the airport, and executed him. Shortly thereafter, Somoza used the National Guard to become dictator of Nicaragua. He and his two sons in succession ruled the country as a virtual family fiefdom for 43 years, and not until the 11th hour—when the Sandinista army was about to take Managua—did the U.S. finally withdraw its support from the Somoza dictatorship.

Companera Mercedes, 25, works in the Nicaraguan prison system for the Ministry of the Interior. She holds a degree in education science from the Autonomous National University of Nicaragua. She joined the Sandinistas in 1973, at age 14, and spent the next few years robbing banks to raise money for the revolution and doing clandestine political organizing in the poor barrios. During the revolution, she was an armed fighter. Her 19-year-old brother is now a militia lieutenant fighting "the mercenaries" in the north, and she has not seen him in over a year.

"I believe a majority of North Americans do not support Reagan's policies," she told me. "I urge them to work to change those policies before it is too late. We do not want war, but we will not give up what we have won. If the Marines come again, they will die." I asked her about the Cuban and Soviet presence in Nicaragua. "The help they provide is help Nicaragua has not been able to get from any other country. Reagan has seen to that. He is waging war against us. We have a right to defend ourselves."

Later the same day, we stopped by a cluster of rundown shacks made of wood, cardboard and tin. A dozen women and small children quickly clustered around us, eager to tell their stories. The land their crude houses stand on was given to them by the government after the revolution, and they receive what amounts to welfare as well, one woman explained, "but it was better before the revolution; things didn't cost so much."

"It doesn't matter what kind of government you have," added an older woman, "so long as you can eat. Now we can't make any money. We can't sell what we want. The government sets the prices and requires permits for everything. People come to Nicaragua and say how beautiful things are. Tell them we are hungry."

I asked them why they were willing to speak so freely. "This hungry child is what makes me speak out," said the first woman. "They may drag me around by the hair, but I don't care. *El hambre es mas hombre que un hombre.* [Hunger is more of a man than any man.]"

As the women talked, a 16-year-old girl with an infant suckling at her breast stood shyly off to one side. She was wearing a cheap bracelet with a pendant likeness of Lenin dangling from it. "Who is that man?" I asked her.

She fingered the pendant for a moment. "I don't know," she replied.

The barrio of Monimbo in the town of Masaya is the place where the final insurrection against Somoza began. The church in the center of town is still heavily pockmarked with bullet holes, and not far from the church is an eloquent statue of a human figure frozen in the act of hurling a paving stone. Paving stones, called *adoquinas,* are a symbol of the revolution.

Many of the roads and streets in Nicaragua are paved with *adoquinas.* After the 1972 earthquake, Somoza decreed that the roads be rebuilt with *adoquinas.* Somoza happened to own the only factory that manufactured *adoquinas.* Seven years later, the people of Nicaragua tore up the streets and built barricades with Somoza's *adoquinas,* from behind which the Sandinista fighters stopped the armored cars of Somoza's National Guard.

Down the street from the scarred church, Peter and I stopped in a small shop to buy some chewing gum. "How much?" Peter asked the teenaged girl who was minding the store.

"Four hundred cordobas."

"That's expensive," said Peter.

"It's not expensive in dollars," she replied with a smile.

Don Alejandro is the local Sandinista representative and leader of a farming co-operative in San Juan de la Concepcion. He joined the FSLN in 1982, after his son was killed fighting the Contras. He is a friend of the Galo family. To reach his house, a one-room structure made of rough planks, tin and tile with a separate cooking shed, we had to drive many kilometers on a narrow dirt road, then walk another three kilometers on a dirt track impassable except for the sturdiest of off-road vehicles.

The land worked by the members of the co-op, Don Alejandro explained, used to belong to large landowners. Much of it went uncultivated while the peasants, working as wage laborers, went hungry. "Our priest told us that God will give us the answer, not the revolution," he said, "but our God is in the countryside. That's where we'll solve our problems. The only people here who are still hungry are those who are not willing to take the land and work it."

Each family in the co-op works its own piece of land, he explained, though the members pool their resources for such things as fertilizer and marketing. As we shared a meal of corn pudding, meat, tortillas and plantain, he explained that the co-op produces coffee, cotton, corn, pineapples, avocados, bananas, rice, mangos, oranges and pitahaya. The co-op's biggest problems are the lack of tractors, road-building and roofing materials.

"Some people think the mercenaries will come and solve all their problems for them," he continued. "They think government price controls are responsible for the food shortages. Here we just work all that much harder, even though our young men have to be away fighting in the north. With hard work, we will defeat those who are trying to undo the revolution. You know who is causing the war in the north, don't you?"

Miguel Vijil, a civil engineer with a degree from Catholic University in Washington, D.C., comes from an old and wealthy family. He used to earn a great deal of money in the petrochemical industry, he told us, but his Catholic beliefs made him uncomfortable about the poverty and suffering he saw all around him. He began doing religious charity work on a case by case basis, but soon came to the conclusion that the only real solution was a total reform of the system — a revolution. Now he is Minister of Housing and Human Settlement in the Nicaraguan government.

"There is little we can do for the squatters here in Managua," he told us, "The countryside must have priority because we don't have the resources to do everything at once. It is not really a problem of urban development, but rather the result of economic distortion endemic to all Central America. You saw Tegucigalpa; it is the same thing there. The way to solve the problem of urban squatters is to rebuild the rural areas, make it desirable for people to return to the land. We lack coffee workers in the countryside while thousands go unemployed here in Managua.

"Before the Contra war began," he continued, "my ministry received 5 percent of the national budget. Now we receive only 2 percent. Yes, we receive aid from the Soviet Union, but that does not make Nicaragua a Soviet stooge. We are a poor country, and we need help. The United States has closed the door on us. Where else can we turn? Mr. Reagan is like the girl who won't dance with a certain boy, then gets angry when the boy dances with another girl."

"But surely the Soviets expect something in return for their aid," I pointed out.

"It is one thing what the Soviets expect in return," he laughed. "It's another thing what Nicaragua will do. Look, we are fighting for our survival. In the history of the world, there has never been a revolution without a counter-revolution. Look at your own revolution. One-third of all the people living in the American colonies left after your revolution; many were forcibly expelled. In Nicaragua, there *were* people who were comfortable under the old regime, and they are not going to be happy when changes are made, but they are a minority. Look at South Africa: if change comes there—and the whole world seems to think that it should—four million people will be unhappy. But the 20 million oppressed have their rights, too. Of course, it is easy to understand South Africa because of the color of people's skin.

"Our only defense is the facts," he concluded. "But the propaganda process in the U.S. is highly professional. Whether our side gets heard in the U.S. media is out of our hands. I don't want a U.S. invasion. Many people will suffer. It is more than my love for Nicaragua and its people. It's my own self-interest that is speaking. I have six children. I want my family to live. We don't ask anything from the United States except to be left alone. That would be enough. It would be a dream come true."

At last we arrive in San Jose de los Remates where we will spend our last night. Peter and I will be staying with Mariano and Rosa Malespin. We are given a small room with two small cots, temporarily evicting the Malespins' 10-year-old son and 8-year-old nephew. Mariano's father will sleep on the table in the front room, beneath a framed picture of Cyndi Lauper. The other seven members of the household will sleep in the main bedroom.

The Malespins live at the edge of the grassy town plaza across from the Catholic church. Up the street is the local militia headquarters. Chickens, pigs, dogs and cows wander through the narrow, rocky, unpaved streets amid houses made of mud and stone. Men on horseback dressed like cowboys ride by. Except for the dim streetlights on most corners, and a black-and-white television set here and there, the town looks like something out of the 19th century. Most of the people in the region make their livings as cattle ranchers or ranch hands, coffee growers and small farmers. Peter and I wander off in search of a beer.

Unfortunately, there doesn't seem to be a single beer left unopened in the whole town. At last, we find what passes for the local saloon—a room, attached to a private home, that contains two tables, half a dozen chairs, a radio blaring popular music in Spanish and English, and a framed poster of Elvis Presley. Three young men are seated at one of the tables drinking a bottle of rum, and they invite us to join them.

They are a farm worker, a teacher, and a dairy milker: 22, 20 and 16 respectively. All three say they are Sandinistas. Almost every young man in Nicaragua is eventually drafted, and we soon discover that the farm worker has just been released from his two-year stint. He spent most of those two years fighting the Contras in the north. The fighting is very heavy, he tells us; six of his friends were killed there. As he talks, his eyes fill with tears.

"*Presidente Reagan es muy loco*," says the teacher, patting his friend on the back. Then he points to their 16-year-old companion. "He doesn't want to fight," he says with a laugh. "He's afraid he'll be killed."

"What about you?" I ask. "Will you go if you're called up?"

"Yes, I will go," the teacher replies. "I expect to be called any day now."

"Aren't you afraid of dying?"

"It doesn't matter if I die," he says. "Only the revolution matters."

Earlier in the afternoon, I had watched Quetzalina playing in the town plaza with a dozen of her San Jose friends, but by now she is fast asleep in her grandparents' house. It is late, and Flavio, Peter, David and I are listening to a recording of Flavio's friend, Carlos Godoy. Tomorrow we *norteamericanos* will head down out of the mountains and return to the United States. As we sip rum and listen to the music, other words than Godoy's come to mind—the words of Major General Smedley Butler, a two-time Congressional Medal of Honor winner.

"I spent 33 years and 4 months in active service as a member of our country's most agile military force—the Marine Corps," General Butler wrote in 1935. "And during that period I spent most of my time being a high-class muscleman for Big Business, for Wall Street and the bankers. In short, I was a racketeer for capitalism.

"Thus I helped make Mexico safe for American oil interests. I helped make Haiti and Cuba decent places for the National Bank boys to collect revenues in. I helped in the raping of half a dozen Central American republics for the benefit of Wall Street. I helped purify Nicaragua for the international banking house of Brown Brothers. I brought light to the Dominican Republic for American sugar interests. I helped make Honduras 'right' for American fruit companies.

"We must give up carrying on offensive warfare and imposing our wills upon other people in distant places," General Butler warned. "Such doctrine is un–American and vicious."

It was incredible testimony, given its source, but it fell on deaf ears. More than 50 years later, and with hardly an interruption in all that time, the government of the United States of America is still carrying on offensive warfare and trying to impose its will upon other people in distant places. And it is all being done in our names and with our tax dollars—and often with our children as well.

"David tells me that you and your wife are expecting a child," says Flavio, interrupting my thoughts.

"Yes," I reply, "in December."

"You must be very happy."

"I'm happy, yes. But I'm also frightened. Your little Queen of Birds is a beautiful child. I hope that my child will never be sent to Nicaragua to wage war against her."

"Thank you, my friend," Flavio replies. "I hope that, too."

ON MEMORIAL DAY

When I was a boy, Memorial Day was my favorite holiday. Its arrival meant that school would soon be over for another year. It was also the day the local swimming pool opened for the summer. Finally, it afforded me the opportunity to decorate my bicycle with red, white and blue crepe paper, and join the big parade down Fifth Street. And the best thing of all was when the American Legion color guard fired its 21-gun salute for America's fallen heroes. That sharp crack was the real thing. Not the adolescent "Bang! Bang!" of our imaginary guns, but the genuine ear-splitting thunder of rifles.

It simply wasn't possible for a 10-year-old to comprehend what Memorial Day really meant. Only when I got to Vietnam as an 18-year-old Marine volunteer did I come to understand that real guns shatter people's skulls and rip their guts to shreds. Only then did I realize that all the pageantry every year is designed to make people believe that it is somehow nobly heroic to send our children off to be maimed, mutilated and butchered.

My grandfather's generation fought in the war to end all wars. My father's generation fought in the war to rid the world of fascists. My generation fought in Vietnam to—to what? What was it for that time? No matter. The killing goes on, as it always has. Since my generation stopped dying in Vietnam, American soldiers have died in Cambodia, Iran, Lebanon, Grenada, and now El Salvador and the Persian Gulf.

And I begin to suspect that the politicians and the generals who tell us that we must sacrifice our children for the cause of peace have gotten their priorities all cockeyed. I didn't see any politicians in the ricefields of Vietnam, and precious few generals died there. Kenny Worman died there. Randy Moore died there. Kids who used to ride their bicycles in Perkasie's Memorial Day parade with me. Kids who had no quarrel with the people who killed them. Kids who died merely because powerful people who would never have to face death in battle told them it was their duty to die.

I don't go to Memorial Day parades anymore. It seems to me that if we really want to honor our fallen soldiers, we might all try a little harder to keep any more of them from falling. It's easy enough to point the finger of blame at another country and say it is all their fault. But it's long past time to realize that the people doing the pointing and the blaming are seldom the ones who end up doing the dying.

STEALING HUBCAPS

Only a few weeks ago, a student where I teach approached me to ask if I would talk to him about the Marine Corps. Seventeen years old, he is just finishing his junior year of high school. He's already made up his mind that he doesn't want to be an enlisted man; he's going to college first, and then he'll become an officer. His dilemma is whether to join the Reserve Officers Training Corps during college, or wait and go through Officer Candidate School after graduation. He wanted to know what I thought.

I asked him why he wants to go into the military at all. He had several answers: to make his resume more attractive when he finally goes looking for a job in the fields of law enforcement or communications; to challenge himself and to gain experience and discipline; to learn hand-to-hand self-defense and to become an expert in the use of firearms. I asked him why he wants to join the Marines. "Because they're the best," he replied. "That's what I want: the best."

I tried to give him a brief history lesson on the uses of U.S. armed forces in the post–World War II era, touching upon such things as the stalemate of Korea, the quagmire of Vietnam, the invasion of the Dominican Republic, the invasion of Grenada, the fiasco in Lebanon, and the attack on the U.S.S. Stark. "Can you give me a good reason why those 265 Marines died in Beirut?" I asked. "Can you give me a good reason for the deaths of those 37 sailors in the Persian Gulf?"

Originally given as the keynote speech at the Conference on Youth, Militarism & Alternatives, Chicago, Illinois, June 3, 1988.

He couldn't. I doubt that he'd ever thought about such questions before. I doubt that he'll ever think about them again. Instead he replied that if he joined ROTC, his college education would be paid for; he could invest the money he would have spent on college and be able to buy his own home a decade sooner than most of his peers.

"What if you don't live that long?" I asked. But the question was meaningless. I've seldom met a teenager who could imagine himself or herself dead, who could conceive of a world without him or her in it. And it is next to impossible to expect a teenager to understand the connections between obscure and distant foreign policy decisions and his or her immediate wants and needs. And taking aim on another human being in combat, let alone killing unarmed middle-aged women or burning some peasant's entire worldly goods, are unfathomable abstractions to those for whom death and misery are confined to newspaper headlines and television adventure shows.

Even as we spoke, our conversation reminded me of a similar conversation I had had with an ex–Marine English teacher of mine fully 22 years ago. I didn't pay any attention to that man, and it was clear early on that this boy wasn't going to pay any attention to me. It was all very frustrating and depressing, but I can't say that I was surprised. Frustration and depression have become chronic conditions of my life.

I could tell you all sorts of horror stories. There was the entire class of first- and second-year college students I had in 1977, none of whom had ever heard of Dean Rusk, much less who he was or what he had been a part of. There was the girl I taught in 1979 who, when confronted with five Vietnam poems in a high school English class, blurted out, "Do we have to read these, Bill? It's so depressing." There was the boy who, in the midst of my 1982 history course on the Vietnam war, asked me when I was going to tell them "the other side," oblivious to the fact that "the other side" is all he's been hearing since the day he was born. But I'm sure all of you have enough horror stories of your own.

I don't know how you deal with your horror stories, but I deal with mine rather poorly. I can't tell you the number of times in the past twenty years that I've wanted to drink myself to death or get a good-paying job in a public relations firm or just crawl under a rock and let the world pass me by. I'm so tired of paddling against the torrent that most days I wake up not knowing how I can possibly pick up the paddle even one more time.

If I could feel like I were getting somewhere, it wouldn't be so bad. But I look around at the world we live in today, and I can't make myself believe that it's any better than the world around me when I was a 17-year-old kid passionately intent upon enlisting in the Marines and utterly oblivious to the irreversible consequences of my decision.

It took a brutal war and a brutal homecoming and a brutal self-examination coupled with a brutal study of history to force me to see the world as I do now. I don't know why I kept at it. I don't know why I didn't end up dead of drugs or suicide, or locked away doing 8-to-20 for aggravated assault with a deadly weapon, or hidden away somewhere deep in the wilderness of the Pacific Northwest, or wrapped in the American flag, parading down Wall Street, crying in my beer and imagining my days in Vietnam as the noblest and most fulfilling experience of my life. A lot of Vietnam veterans did. I don't know why, but I didn't.

Instead, I came to the messianic and naive conviction that Vietnam might end up being worth something good after all, that out of the debacle could grow the seeds of a new understanding, not just for me, but for my country. I believed it because I wanted to believe it, because I didn't know what else to believe.

But the war dragged on and on and on. Most of the once-vast anti-war movement dried up and blew away like dead leaves in November long before the war finally ground to an end nearly a decade after I had fought there. Gerald Ford pardoned Richard Nixon, but he wouldn't pardon those who'd resisted what had long since become Richard Nixon's war. Jimmy Carter offered resisters a deal that wasn't much better, and no deal at all for military deserters and veterans with "bad paper discharges." Ronald Reagan declared the Vietnam war a noble cause, and the vast momentum of our collective national mythology has worked hard and with great success to fix that assessment as the final verdict of history.

It's really much worse than that. Nuclear stockpiles are geometrically larger than they were even 15 years ago. Our government has replaced the blood-price of American lives in Vietnam with the far less politically costly dollar-price of low-intensity conflict all over Central America. We are daily confronted with such absurdities as U.S.-backed guerrillas attacking U.S.-owned oil refineries in Angola, U.S.-sponsored Afghan rebels who think the Ayatollah Khomeini is the best invention since ice cream, and U.S. recognition of the genocidal Pol Pot regime as the legitimate government of Cambodia. We've got the same bunch of cloak-and-dagger men who once equipped an army of Lao mercenaries by selling heroin to American GI's in Saigon equipping an army of Nicaraguan mercenaries by selling cocaine in the streets of our own cities.

Most disturbing of all is that the American people, most of them at least, just sit there day after day and year after year and let it all happen. How in the world are we going to get teenagers to understand the world they live in when we can't even get grown people to learn enough or care enough or think enough to do it? And what really scares me is that I find myself more and more forgiving of my fellow citizens. Fifteen years ago, I couldn't even talk to such people without shouting. Ten years ago, I couldn't understand why everyone wasn't busily reading *WIN* magazine and *The Nation* and *Bury My Heart at Wounded Knee*.

But if the world hasn't changed much in 20 years, I surely have. The past eight years, in particular, have brought a personal "revolution" about which I have deeply ambivalent feelings. In 1981, I got married. In 1985, after two decades of living in barracks and dormitories, out of the backs of cars and on other people's livingroom sofas, or in rented apartments, I bought a house. In 1986, my wife and I had a child. More and more, my life has taken on the shapes and rhythms of so many Americans for whom I once harbored nothing but contempt.

I've got responsibilities now. My wife and my child deserve something better than sleeping bags and canned sardines. I've got bills to pay, a rotting back stair that needs to be fixed, a hamper perpetually full of dirty clothes, and a widowed mother who'll break her neck if she tries to change her own storm windows. I've got a classroom full of 15-year-olds who'll eat me alive the first day I come into school unprepared. I can't even find the time to keep up with my own writing, let alone to go out and change the world.

And I *care*. I've given most of my adult life to the struggle that brings us here tonight. I know what it means to be cannon fodder. But you tell me where I'm supposed to get the time or the energy to read the latest issue of *NACLA Report*, or attend the next meeting of Pledge of Resistance, or leaflet the reservists at Willow Grove Naval Air Station.

It isn't anger that I feel so much anymore, though I am certainly angry, but rather a marrow-deep sadness heavy as cast iron. Henry Kissinger gets $15,000 every time he opens his mouth. G. Gordon Liddy stars on *Miami Vice*. Sylvester Stallone earns multi-millions refighting a war in Hollywood that he desperately avoided in real life. And I end up feeling guilty about the $200 I've been paid to come here and talk to people who already think pretty much like me. Each year I move more slowly, read less avidly, turn down more unpaid work, and believe less passionately that anything I have ever done or ever will do will make one damned bit of difference.

Even as I write this, my daughter has been crying inconsolably for nearly an hour. Do I stop writing and try to comfort her, or do I let my wife bear all the burden of coping with a teething 18-month-old? At least my wife understands what I'm doing. How do I explain to my daughter that I don't have time for her because I have to inspire a group of people intent upon tilting at windmills? All she will know of this day is that her father wasn't there when she needed him. And each time I choose to spend what little spare time I have in trying to make a better world for my daughter, I am putting that much more distance between myself and my child, losing that much more of the precious little time I have to give to her and to receive the blessing of her tears. And I want more than ever just to put the world aside and live my life in peace.

But of course, there's the catch: whatever peace I might find by ignoring the world around me is and always will be no more than an illusion, a luxury of place and time and circumstance, a buy-now-pay-later sort of proposition that may one day come back at me with a vengeance too terrible to contemplate. How long before all those thousands of nuclear weapons are finally triggered? What happens when the rain forests are finally gone? What will I say to my students when they come back and ask me, "Why didn't anyone tell us?" What will I say to my daughter when she explains to me that she can get a college education and learn valuable life skills if she enlists in the army?

That's the trouble with knowledge: once you've learned something, it's hard to unlearn it. Once you've seen the misery of others, it's hard to believe that such misery will never be yours, or your children's or your grandchildren's. Once you've seen the world for what it is, it's hard to ignore it. And once you've seen the world for what it could be, it's hard to accept it for what it is.

This is what is known as being stuck between a rock and a hard place. Nothing I do will make any difference, but to do nothing requires a kind of amnesia I have yet to discover a means of inducing. The dilemma leaves me much of the time feeling like a failure at everything I do. Certainly it requires only the most rudimentary powers of observation to notice that I haven't had much success at changing the world. Meanwhile, I don't spend enough time on my teaching, I don't spend enough time on my writing, I don't spend enough time with my wife, and I don't spend enough time with my daughter. Jack of all trades; master of none.

But what else can I do? A rock and a hard place. So I bumble along like a punchdrunk boxer too broken to win and too proud to go down for the count. Some days are better than others. On my bad days, I am somewhat less sociable than a Kodiak bear with a toothache. On my bad days, those horror stories of mine hide in the shadows quietly laughing at me, and there are shadows everywhere I look.

But I do have good days, too. And on those good days, I draw strength and inspiration from people like Lou Ann Merkle, who conceived and brought into being what has got to be the most remarkable comic book in history, *Real War Stories.* People like Brian Willson, who lost his legs but not his heart. People like Jan Barry, who single-handedly created the first county-level peace commission in the United States. People like Rick and Laura Quiggle, who are raising five children on a blue-collar salary while refusing to accept the collective complacency of the entire city of Erie. People like Martin Sheen, who donated the entire proceeds from his part in the movie *Gandhi* to Sister Mother Teresa. People like my own students, who recently collected an entire truckload of clothing and school supplies for the children of Nicaragua. People like, well, all of you. Ordinary people, just as tired and harried and over-extended as I am, who somehow find the courage and the will to do the extraordinary. And to keep doing it in the face of certain failure.

That young student of mine will probably end up joining the Marines, and I'm sorry I couldn't figure out a way to be a bit more persuasive with him. Maybe next time I'll get it right. Or the time after that. Every once in awhile, I actually do get it right. There was the former student of mine in 1983 who was all set to join ROTC in college, but didn't. "I kept thinking about things you'd said in class," he told me. "I just couldn't make myself sign the papers." There was the phone call I got in 1985 from a 22-year-old unemployed bricklayer from Brooklyn who was just about to enlist in the Air Force when he read my book *Vietnam–Perkasie*. He'd just called to say that he'd changed his mind about enlisting. There was the woman from Texas who told me after reading my book *Passing Time*, "I feel as if I've made a friend, someone on this earth who has touched my soul and said what I've been feeling for a long time." And there was the letter I received in 1987 from a 16-year-old high school boy in Seattle who said, "I guess you could say I'm really trying to understand what went on during Vietnam and why. I've been watching the Iran-Contra hearings, and it seems like one big mess. Anyway, Bill, you have sure changed my perspective on a lot of things and I'm really glad I've read your books."

Things like that don't happen as often as I would like them to happen, but they do happen. And I'm sharing them with you not because you need to hear them, but because I need to hear them. Too often, I am too caught up in my own weariness and frustration and self-pity to take the time to consider the people for whom I *have* made a difference.

I no longer believe that I can change the world. I no longer believe that even all of us together are going to change the world. But I do believe that we have to keep trying because if our voices fall silent, the only voices left will be those of people like Elliot Abrams and Oliver North. I have to keep trying because it is the only way I can live with myself, knowing what I know. It is the only way I can live with my wife, who believes in me more than I believe in myself. It is the only way I can live with my daughter, who will inherit the world I give her.

I'll tell you my darkest fantasy: when they drop the big bomb on the oil refineries of South Philadelphia, I want to have time to take my daughter in my arms and hold her tight and whisper into her ear, "Kid, I'm sorry about this. I did the best I could." That's it. That's all I ask for. Looking around at the world through rational eyes, that's all I reasonably *can* ask for: the time to say it, and the knowledge that what I am saying is true, that I did the best I could.

And who knows? Maybe I'm wrong. It wouldn't be the first time.

Maybe it isn't as bad as I think. Maybe we really can change the world. I know one thing for sure: I certainly can't do it without you. If you're willing to keep trying, so am I. What else are we going to do with ourselves, anyway? Steal hubcaps?

ON *The Genre of Silence*

In 1937, with the Soviet Union firmly in the grip of Joseph Stalin, the *Yezhovshchina* or Great Terror began. "Thousands are executed," writes Duncan Bush, "millions arrested and deported to concentration camps. Among those who 'disappear' are intellectuals, Red Army leaders and former revolutionaries. Over the next decade of Stalin's rule, among those groups most systematically subjected to repression, arrest, imprisonment and death are writers."

One of those writers was a poet named Victor Bal, little known in his own time, unheard of today. Born in Petersburg in 1898, the son of a doctor, Bal attended the same school as Osip Mandelstam and Vladimir Nabokov, but his later studies at Petersburg University were interrupted, apparently permanently, by the October Revolution. He fought on the side of the Bolsheviks in the Civil War until he was disabled with a knee injury in 1920. Subsequently, he settled in Moscow, where he began working on film scripts. A member of the Writers' Union, he was sent into exile somewhere east of the Ural Mountains in 1937, and all trace of him disappears after the spring of 1938.

What little we know of him, offered by Welsh poet Bush for the first time in English in *The Genre of Silence* (Poetry Wales Press, Bridgend), comes from fifteen finished poems and a handful of unfinished fragments and drafts, a few pages from Bal's civil war journal, a short autobiographical essay, notes from a series of interviews with Bal conducted by Yevgeni Nikolayevich Gubski in 1937, and a much later interview with Aleksandr Stepanov, who had known Bal peripherally in the 1920s. Out of these scant fragments,

Bush manages not only to resurrect a vanished life, but to recreate on an intimately human scale two of the most cataclysmic events of the 20th century.

Bal's surviving body of poetry is simply too small to allow for generalizations, let alone to attempt to judge him against such contemporaries of his as Mandelstam and Isaac Babel. (There is evidence that Bal published at his own expense a book-length collection of poetry called *Sunflowers* in 1922, but no surviving copy has yet surfaced.) What there is, however, suggests a poet of great sensitivity and subtle power. A poet, like Mandelstam or Pablo Neruda or Rubin Dario, honest enough and courageous enough to be dangerous. As Mandelstam's wife, Nadezhda, once said, "People can be killed for poetry here—a sign of unparalleled respect—because they are capable of living by it." Such respect, it seems, was given to Bal.

Of the poems themselves, three apparently predate the revolution. "The Galley" is a thinly veiled condemnation of Czarist government. "Summer. Evening" is a bucolic revery. "For Marina" is a love poem so tender it seems out of place amid the destruction of war and the politics of terror that fuel the later poems. He writes that his lover's body is:

> ...so long and beautiful
> sometimes it hurts my heart
>
> and makes my eyes
> flinch almost so I have to look
>
> away, as from a mirror
> flashing all the sun into my face.

Five poems deal with the Civil War, with Bal's comrades and with the hapless peasants who are always the earth upon which armies tred. Though Bal was a Bolshevik by choice, the poems are empty of politics and ideology, conveying instead only the sadness and the cost of war. "What we come upon," he writes in "Black Smoke":

> or leave are dead and dying.
> And only in mythology
> can Daphne change into a tree.

In "Archaic Profile," about a soldier who has had his nose shot off, Bal reflects:

Who can explain these things?
And why try, when death already
chafes us no more than an old boot?
***
The best that Besmanov will hope for now
is not to lose his nose in one corner
of the Ukraine and his body,
six weeks later, in another.

In "Toy Soldier," Bal manages a double irony: that a soldier would waste precious bullets to make a child's toy, and that the toy should be a lead soldier. In "Peasant Burial,"

. . . the second-born is borne

in a child's small coffin
in her brother's washed white nightdress
still and now forever too big for her.

That Bal consciously considered, and rejected, any sense of the "heroic" in these poems, that he was doubtful whether the ends justified the means, is suggested by an unfinished draft in his journal. "Now pawns trudge mud/ to mindlessness, slewing up/ stolen field guns to defend or/ take an empty square," he writes. Two stanzas later, he seems to try to elevate the war to an overtly ideological level. "The white Red blood/has had to melt[,]" he begins to say, but these last two lines are crossed out, as if he could not reconcile the pedestrian mindlessness of mud and the struggle for an empty square with some abstract and ultimately romantic image of blood melting—be it Bolshevik blood or not. At last, he abandons the poem unfinished.

The finished poems are consequently universal: they might have been written about any war, and they are deeply moving. That they lack "proletarian heroism" or "socialist realism" may help to explain why Bal did not find much success with the Soviet state publishing houses. Quietly "subversive" as the civil war poems may be, however, the seven later poems, all apparently written in 1937, are both politically barbed and courageously bitter. If the civil war poems made Bal suspect, these later poems must surely have sealed his fate.

In "Writers' Union Building, Moscow, 1937," Bal describes the members of the union as "[S]heep/ milling for the microphone/ like wolves. And, like wolves, getting/ stronger the longer you run."

I

In "The Leader," he pokes holes in Stalin's ruthless vanity while articulating the danger he faces by doing so, acknowledging "the future/some of us won't see." He speaks of "the times'/skullduggery and paranoia" in "The Age of Rust." Not only the physical cost, but also the awesome psychological cost of Stalin's Great Terror is hauntingly conveyed in "Night, Day":

> We lie awake at night and dream
> the knocking at the door through which
> we'll disappear for ever. By day, commune
> our fate and share deliverance with
>
> surprising crowds left on the pavements still.
> By the Kremlin wall, too, a queue lengthens
> in patience, as if to view
> the calf's blood and pig's bones
>
> of Christ. While with every swivel-perfect
> change of guard, even Lenin,
> waxen in the mausoleum, thinks
> that they have come for him at last.

And then came the knocking at the door through which Victor Bal disappeared forever, and only through the chance discovery of a hatbox that had once belonged to Gubski do we have any knowledge that Bal ever existed. Y. N. Gubski, the failed poet, who survived the Terror only to die by suicidal hanging in 1954. Gubski, who once tried to publish "The Galley" as his own work. As Bush observes: "Out of the past that is irrevocable, it is one of the ironies of historical and biographical research that isolated facts or grounds for compelling supposition emerge, when they do, in so random and irrelevant a form."

In that hatbox was found most of the material which comprises *The Genre of Silence*. To this material, Bush has added the interview with Stepanov, which was recorded in the geriatric wing of a Leningrad hospital in 1987, a few historical annotations to the poems, and some material by and about Mandelstam and Babel that helps to clarify comments Bal made to Gubski during their 1937 interviews.

One learns, for instance, that the five bullets in "Toy Soldier" is a reference to Bal's habit of keeping one chamber empty to prevent accidental discharge of his pistol. And "Peasant" takes on a deeper meaning when one reads this entry from Bal's civil war journal: "A sickle sharpened on a fieldstone, hour by hour for centuries: that's what they are. They've been here so long they think they'll outlive the world." The inspiration for "Black Smoke" lies in a journal entry dated August 19, 1918: "A mother, grandmother and daughter — probably no more than fourteen — whom we found gang-raped (no doubt was possible) then bayoneted upon the same hut floor." Then, on August 20: "I kept thinking afterwards of the lordly jokes the Greeks made about Zeus's satyriasis. Iope having to change into a cow to get away from him, Daphne into a laurel tree. That stuff won't work now, not any more."

The interview material that Gubski recorded is equally fascinating, illuminating the Stalin-era poems less directly but no less powerfully. When asked by Gubski why he wrote so little, Bal replied, "What do you want me to say? A real poet, after all, can be judged by the poems he rejects or abandons just as much as by those he chooses or is lucky enough to find a publisher for." Yet that measured and artistically couched response demonstrates the tension between honesty and survival faced by anyone in Bal's uneasy position, especially when one compares Bal's reply to his own unfinished poem, "Geranium":

> You must, I tell myself,
> live slow and sure and silent
> and within yourself. Act
> blind and deaf and
> dumb. Above all, dumb.
> Shape words, but give forth
> silence.

It was Babel, speaking at the 1934 Writers' Congress, who described himself as "the master of the genre of silence." But Bal understood, as well as Babel, that to say anything at all was dangerous. As Bal wrote in a poem for Mandelstam, referring to a then-unpublished poem of Mandelstam's:

> Safer, you thought, in days
> like these, to live a bird
> then as a man,
> pretending to forget that
> cagebirds sing, and can be heard.

Indeed, there were politics and danger even in a goldfinch, for as Bal pointed out to Gubski, "That bird's not a stuffed bird. It isn't a vulture in a case."

Yet even silence offered no safety, as both Babel and Bal must surely have understood. Bal tells Gubski of a chance encounter he had with Babel on the night Babel spoke of the genre of silence: "He looked drained, empty. I thought it was a look I'd seen on soldiers at the front. After an attack, or sometimes just from sheer exhaustion, you'd suddenly notice a man looked like a corpse. As if he were already dead. 'He's gone,' we used to say. 'He's just waiting to stiffen up.' Babel would have understood what I meant by that."

One can only wonder if Bal was thinking of himself as he spoke. "What I suppose I'm trying to say," he told Gubski, "is that you look for a pattern in all these things, some higher meaning. Until you realize that there's only one meaning and it's this: that's how things are for us. We're one of those generations. We weren't born in a bed just so we could die in one."

And, like millions of others, Bal did not. Instead he disappeared into the vast wilderness of Siberia and simply vanished for fifty years. That he has not vanished forever is a matter of fortuitous chance coupled with the extraordinary talent of Duncan Bush, an accomplished poet in his own right and the author of three previous books (*Aquarium, Salt,* and *Black Faces, Black Mouths*).

The Genre of Silence is part poetry, part history, and part mystery. Yes, there's a mystery here, though one I am not at liberty to reveal. What I *can* say is that while the book deals with specific events and specific people, it speaks clearly to the timelessness of war, repression and resistance, brutality and resilience. If the indomitable human spirit is a cliche, it is nevertheless what finally and triumphantly remains of the life of Victor Bal, and the lives of the nameless millions all over the world, now and for all times, that Victor Bal represents.

A LETTER TO MCGEORGE BUNDY

In the spring of 1966, at age seventeen, I enlisted in the United States Marine Corps. Lyndon Johnson had only recently warned the American people that if we did not stop the communists in Vietnam, we would one day have to fight them on the sands of Waikiki, and the words of John Kennedy were still reverberating in my heart as if he'd spoken them directly to me: "Ask not what your country can do for you; ask what you can do for your country." I was going to serve my country in Vietnam.

I had never heard of Archimedes Patti or Christian de Castries, Edward Lansdale or the Binh Xuyen. I did not know that China had occupied Vietnam for a thousand years, or that Ho Chi Minh had sought and been refused an audience with Woodrow Wilson at Versailles. I knew only what was necessary to do my job: How to fire and clean my rifle, how to apply a pressure bandage to a sucking chest wound, how to make a stove from an empty C-ration can.

Whether the United States should have been in Vietnam or not was a question I never asked myself before I arrived there. That was not part of my job. That was the job of men like Lyndon Johnson, Dean Rusk, Robert McNamara, McGeorge Bundy and Walt Rostow, and I trusted my government leaders, elected and appointed, to do their job just as I was doing mine.

There is an implicit but sacred bargain struck between those who ask others to put their lives at risk and those who do the risking, and for those who do the risking, it goes like this: I will give you my life to do with what you will so long as your cause is worthy of my sacrifice. I accepted that bargain willingly, proudly, because

135

those who put me at risk assured me and my country that the cause was indeed worthy.

During the long and painful passage of the thirteen months I fought in Vietnam, however, I found myself less and less confident that either I or my government knew what we were doing. In a world of free fire zones and Bouncing Betty mines, punji pits and Zippo raids, it became increasingly difficult to believe in anything but my own survival. In a world where helpless old men were beaten bloody and small children were included in the body count of Viet Cong dead, it became impossible to avoid the conclusion that I was fundamentally, perhaps pathologically, evil.

By the time I left Vietnam in the waning days of the Tet Offensive and the battle for Hue, I had become acutely aware that something had gone horribly wrong in Vietnam. But I didn't know what. I thought maybe it was me. Men like Rusk and Bundy and Rostow were still insisting that the cause was worthy. They would soon be replaced by men like Richard Nixon and Henry Kissinger, but these men, too, would insist the worthiness of their cause right up to the very moment North Vietnamese tanks crushed the gates of the Presidential Palace in Saigon, achieving at an incalculable cost in human suffering what might have been achieved without the loss of a single life thirty years earlier.

I paid a terrible price for the bargain I struck with the people who sent me to wage war on Vietnam: more than a decade of nightmares and alcohol and self-loathing; a white-hot fury, shapeless and unpredictable, that seared anyone who came too close; a loneliness profound as the silence between the stars. And I was lucky.

I have friends whose names are carved into that ugly black slab in Washington, D.C. I have friends who were dumped into wheelchairs at nineteen and won't be taken out again until they are laid into their coffins. I have friends who still can't see an Asian face without trembling. I have friends who live in shacks deep in the forests of the Olympic Peninsula. I have friends whose wives are afraid to touch them when they are sleeping.

Okay. My friends and I made a mistake and we paid the price. I've learned to accept my share of responsibility for that mistake. I can live with myself. But where now are the people who asked us to take the risks? Where have they been these past twenty years? Willy Crapser spent seventeen years in and out of psychiatric wards, and Robert McNamara became president of the World

Bank. Ron Kovic never had the chance to have children before he was paralyzed for life, and McGeorge Bundy became president of the Ford Foundation. Kenny Worman and Randy Moore have been dead longer than they got to live, and Walt Rostow and Dean Rusk are respected professors at respected universities.

Not once, not once in all these years, have I ever heard a single high-level policymaker of the Vietnam war apologize for what he did, ever admit that he made a mistake, ever show the slightest sign of remorse for all the havoc and misery, the shattered lives and shattered families and shattered nations left gasping in the wake of his decisions. There is no regret, no sorrow, no shame. Some of these men merely skulked off the public stage quietly. Others continue to this day to insist that their cause was worthy, and is worthy, and always will be worthy.

Honorable men, they asked my friends and me to get down and dirty in the ricefields only to abandon us under fire. We did the killing and the dying, and then they left us to find our own way back while they went on with their honorable lives as if nothing at all were out of order. They struck a bargain with us, and then they broke it. And they have refused ever after to admit that it was broken.

I have often wondered how these men live with themselves. How do they get up each day and look themselves in the eye? How do they go on pretending that God's in His heaven, all's right with the world? Or are there private doubts, private demons, they are simply too proud or too ashamed to admit?

Five years ago, I happened to attend a meeting held in the political science building at New York University. Someone told me that McGeorge Bundy was teaching there. In an idle moment during a coffee break, I checked the faculty mailboxes and there it was: a small cubbyhole, like all the others, marked by a small typed tab: McGeorge Bundy. The man the *Pentagon Papers* called the major architect of the Vietnam war. Reasoning that this was likely as close as I would ever get to any of the men with whom I'd struck that fateful bargain years ago, I took the opportunity then and there to write Bundy a short letter. It read something like this:

> Dear Mr. Bundy,
>   Couldn't you just once in all these years have taken the time to apologize? Couldn't you just once have said, "I'm sorry. We

made a mistake." Couldn't you just once admit that you were wrong?

> Sincerely yours,
> William D. Ehrhart
> formerly Sergeant, USMC
> Vietnam 1967–68

I included my address and telephone number, too, but I never received a reply. Well, it was a Saturday afternoon in early summer. It was an open mailbox accessible to anyone. Maybe he didn't get my letter. Maybe he was on vacation. Maybe some secretary threw it away.

But the questions I asked in that letter are not so easily discarded. Not by me, at least. So I'm going to try again:

> Dear Mr. Bundy,
>
> Couldn't you just once in all these years have taken the time to apologize? Couldn't you just once have said, "I'm sorry. We made a mistake." Couldn't you just once admit that you were wrong? I'd like to believe that you and your friends are not evil, but only human. I'd like to believe that you didn't just walk away from the wreckage you created without a second thought. I'd like to believe that you have nightmares too.
>
> Do you? I'd really like to know.

ON FLAG-BURNING

This past July, I almost got the chance to testify before Congress. The House Judiciary Committee's Subcommittee on Civil Rights was holding hearings on the burning issue of flag-burning, and a staff aide called to ask if I, as a veteran and writer, might be willing to appear. "Sure," I said, "I am not now, nor have I ever been. . . ."

The question before the committee was whether to amend the Constitution in order to ensure respect for the flag, or merely to enact a federal statute. Sadly for me, the issue was ultimately deemed too important to be left in the hands of a lightweight with only a Purple Heart and a handful of poems. The heavyweights were called up: a former prisoner of war, a Medal of Honor winner, a National Book Award winner, and the redoubtable Col. Harry Summers, Ret.

I'm still not sure who won the bout. There will be no constitutional amendment, for the moment at least, but it is now — or shortly will be — a federal crime to desecrate the flag.

Only last week, I saw a woman jogging along Philadelphia's Kelly Drive; she was wearing red-and-white-striped shorts, and the left rear panel was blue with white stars. No doubt about it: an American flag! And the brazen hussy was sweating all over it. If she tries to pull that stunt next week, will the Flag Police leap out from behind the statue of Leif Ericson and bundle her off to jail?

The next time Crazy Larry from Crazy Larry's Used Cars gets on UHF in his red-white-and-blue Stars & Stripes Uncle Sam suit and tells me it's my patriotic duty to buy, buy, buy at the lowest prices in the Used Car War, will the Flag Police snatch him off the air?

139

What does it mean to desecrate the flag, anyway? Truth be told, I've never seen Old Glory looking more beautiful or inspiring than it did girdling the hips of that lovely young jogger. On the other hand, I find myself repulsed by the multitude of obscenities the flag is subjected to in the endless frenzy to part me from my hard-earned wages. Desecration, like beauty, is in the eyes of the beholder.

And the beholders who count will be the cops, the prosecutors, the judges, and the juries. Just what our legal system needs, already overburdened as it is to the point of being dysfunctional.

And of course, all this will cost tax dollars, which brings me to another point. How much money has Congress spent calling possible witnesses; transporting, feeding and lodging the honored Chosen; transcribing and publishing testimony? How many labor-hours have been spent listening to expert testimony, debating and declaiming, drafting legislation? It's a sure bet that guy who called me wasn't working for free.

Meanwhile, my wife can't walk three blocks from Market East Station to her job without being confronted daily with the facts of joblessness and homelessness in the United States. We can't allow our daughter to play unsupervised in broad daylight on our neighborhood playground in East Mount Airy. My mother has to live with the constant fear that what little security she has managed to scrape together in a lifetime may be wiped out overnight by a single illness.

And Congress is wasting its time, money and energy trying to decide whether or not James Madison got it right?

I would have said these things to the House Judiciary Subcommittee on Civil Rights. I would have told them, "Shame on you. Haven't you got anything better to do with yourselves? Can't you guys get real for once?"

I'm sure I would have been persuasive. I'm sure I would have sent them all scurrying back to their offices suitably chastened and ready to get down to business. But I never got the chance.

So now we have this new law. And the funny thing is that the President isn't happy with it. He doesn't think it's tough enough. He thinks James Madison really did get it wrong. Madison wasn't patriotic enough.

This is the same President who says he's got nothing against the Panamanian Defense Forces, as though Manuel Noriega could spend several decades drug trafficking and money laundering without another soul in his army knowing what he's been up to. Like Noriega has been doing all this in his spare time, using the family sedan.

This is the same President whose brand new "War on Drugs" is essentially a reprise of the plan Richard Nixon tried with no success almost two decades ago: Let's get tough, put 'em all in jail. Maybe he hasn't heard that here in Philadelphia we're already letting criminals *out* of jail because there's no more room at the inn.

This is the same President who was Number Two Man in an administration that, according to *Drugs, Law Enforcement and Foreign Policy* (U.S. Government Printing Office, 1989), deliberately impeded the fight against drugs to combat what they perceived to be the greater threat of Communism in Latin America.

Our streets are flowing with drugs, our children are drowning in drugs, and the President and his pals think that's less important than defending our shores against the godless Sandinistas and their Marxist minions in the coffee fields. This is patriotism?

But Congress and the President want me to respect the flag, and they're going to see that I do, even if they have to put me in prison. Well, there's certainly going to be no more flag-burning around my house. Hey, I'm no dummy. I can take a hint.

The absence of flag-burning, however, doesn't necessarily ensure respect for the flag, or the principles and the Republic for which it stands. Respect is something that is earned.

When our public schools are falling apart, and the President calls a summit conference on education to which not a single teacher is invited, it does not engender respect.

When Congress authorizes development of B-2 bombers at $500,000,000 per plane while eliminating my mother's catastrophic health insurance, it does not engender respect.

When kids know they can make more money in one year by selling crack than they could ever dream of making by a whole lifetime of honest labor, it does not engender respect.

And when the substance of freedom is subverted by a hypocritical genuflection to the symbols of freedom, we're all in a whole lot of trouble.

If Congress and the President would stop their perpetual posturing and start dealing with some of the real issues that confront our nation, perhaps fewer people would have to be coerced into respecting the flag.

TEACHING THE VIETNAM WAR

"His voice trailed off as though it were the end of an early-morning party, with wine bottles and beer bottles lined up along the windowsills and across the floor and everybody out of cigarettes."

Imagine the man who belongs to that voice. What do you conjure? Bone-deep physical exhaustion, perhaps. A soul too weary for anything but a kind of hollow resignation. The party's over, but there is nowhere else to go, nothing to look forward to. All that remains, like lingering cigarette smoke and the odor of stale alcohol floating heavily in the still air, is silence, thick and deep and all but impenetrable.

That sentence, buried in the early pages of Larry Heinemann's superb novel of the Vietnam war, *Close Quarters*, is, in my estimation, one of the most powerful and evocative sentences pen ever put to paper. In thirty-five words, Heinemann graphically offers readers a frightening glimpse of the cost of war, the toll war takes on the human psyche. It is a hard nugget of truth, capable of breaking teeth and impossible to swallow whole. One cannot read sentences like that without being brought up short, without confronting the reality behind the generations of mythology and rhetoric that propel young men (and now women, too) to the killing fields. Indeed, if one wants to know the essence of war, how it feels and smells and tastes, what it does to those who are scorched by its flames, one is likely to find more truth in literature than in any history ever written.

But of course, most people today read neither history nor literature. In my class on Vietnam War Literature this past semester, I took a poll on the first day: fewer than half a dozen students had ever read a book about the Vietnam war. But every single student in the class had seen at least half a dozen commercial movies about the war. And for most of my students, all but one under the age of 35, those movies, together with several popular television shows and a few vague childhood memories, constituted the sum total of their knowledge about the most turbulent event in U.S. history since the Civil War.

For those of us who lived through those years, especially those of us who came of age during those years and were deeply affected by Vietnam, it seems impossible that the stuff and substance of our lives could be for others nothing more than history, as remote and inaccessible as the siege of Troy, perceived only through the distorted lens of the glitz-and-glitter world of Hollywood. But succeeding generations cannot absorb the experience of previous generations by osmosis.

That is why I teach the Vietnam war. I think it is important. I think people ought to know what happened and why. Here is the course I taught this past semester for the William Joiner Center at the University of Massachusetts at Boston (I taught it as a literature course, but it can just as easily be taught as history using virtually the same materials):

I begin my course with a history book: George Herring's *America's Longest War*. Because my students generally know nothing worth knowing about Vietnam, it is essential to offer them at least enough basic history to allow them to place the literature into some kind of historical context. We read Herring a chapter or two at a time, just prior to whichever book corresponds to that period of the war. I have disagreements with Herring; I would prefer to use Michael Maclear's *The Ten Thousand Day War*, but it is too massive and detailed to use in conjunction with the eight additional books I assign. Herring's book is the best short history that I have come across.

After reading Herring's chapter on the French Indochina War, we begin the literature with Graham Greene's novel *The Quiet American*, set in 1952 and written in 1954. This book is undoubtedly the most remarkable book ever written about the war. That an English journalist could see so clearly and dispassionately the whole terrible disaster into which the United States even then was so energetically and blindly hurling itself is only slightly less amazing than the fact that no one who mattered paid the slightest attention to Greene's warning.

Next we read Tran Van Dinh's *No Passenger on the River*, a novel set mostly in Vietnam in 1963, and written within a year after the overthrow of Ngo Dinh Diem, which is the climax of the book. Long out of print, Dinh's book was just republished in 1989. In the past, I have used Smith Hempstone's *A Tract of Time*, which deals with the same period, but Dinh's book offers the advantage of a Vietnamese point of view, something that remains hard to come by in the literature available in English. The students also read the poetry of Jan Barry, who served in Vietnam as a young enlisted soldier in 1962. (All the poetry in the course is taken from *Carrying the Darkness: The Poetry of the Vietnam War*, Texas Tech University Press, 1989.)

Larry Heinemann's *Close Quarters*, set in 1967–68, comes next. This is perhaps the hardest selection to make because the overwhelming majority of books about the war are written by veterans and deal with the American combat experience. Many of these books, both novels and memoirs, are very good. (One thinks immediately of Philip Caputo's *A Rumor of War* or Tim O'Brien's *Going After Cacciato*.) But "the Vietnam experience," it seems to me, is in fact much larger than the simple story of American boys slogging through the paddy fields, however compelling that story may be. One book on that aspect of the war is enough. And if I can only use one, it has to be *Close Quarters*.

All through the 1980s, as the public image of the Vietnam veteran was transformed from drug-crazed psychopath to cultural icon, I have been wondering how long the rest of the "Vietnam generation" would stand silently on the sidelines, allowing popular culture to obliterate the fact that the overwhelming majority of my generation did not serve in Vietnam, though many were nevertheless touched, and sometimes deeply affected, by the war. Finally, in 1988, *Saigon, Illinois* appeared. The novel's author, Paul Hoover, was a legal conscientious objector during the war who did alternative service in a Chicago hospital. The book is funny, sensitive and honest, giving at last a credible voice to those who chose not to go, or at least to one significant segment of that group. In conjunction with *Saigon, Illinois,* we also read poems by others of my generation who did not go: Christopher Bursk, Charles Fishman, James Moore, Bill Tremblay and Tom Wayman.

It is a little awkward, for me and my students both, to teach my own writing, but I do, and it is usually very rewarding and enlightening for all of us. The book I use most often is *Passing Time*, a nonfiction memoir that covers the years immediately after I returned from Vietnam, roughly 1969–74. While there is no shortage of books about the combat experience, as I said, books which deal at length with the aftermath of the war for those who fought it are still relatively few (one of the best is William Crapser's extended short story "Wild Child," which appears in his collection *Remains*), and that part of the experience is important, as any vet will tell you: in Vietnam, no matter how bad things got, you could always look forward to your rotation date, but once you got back to The World, there you were, and you just had to get by as best you could. It wasn't easy, and for many vets, the passing years have not made it any easier.

By this time, we've read all of Herring, chapter by chapter, and we move on to a concentrated discussion of the poetry of John Balaban, D. F. Brown, Horace Coleman, Bryan Alec Floyd, Yusef Komunyakaa, Walter McDonald, Basil T. Paquet and Bruce Weigl. Long before they reach college, most students are convinced that poetry is either boring or inaccessible or both. But I can't teach a Vietnam course without resorting to poetry. The poetry written about Vietnam is both plainspoken and eloquent. If your students think they don't like poetry, or can't understand it, have them read some of this stuff; it'll blow their socks off.

Vietnam affected women, too, in all sorts of ways, and I try to reflect that in my course. The book I use is Bobbie Ann Mason's *In Country*. Though women's literature on the war is still relatively sparse, I could easily have chosen Lynda Van Devanter's *Home Before Morning*, Patricia Walsh's *Forever Sad the Hearts*, or one of several oral histories about women in Vietnam. I chose Mason's novel, set in Kentucky in 1984, because its teenaged female protagonist is endearing and believable, because Mason's treatment of veterans is thoughtful and sympathetic, and because Mason understands intrinsically the frightening fluidity of the boundary between reality and contemporary popular culture. The ending is too easy, but you can't always have everything.

Speaking of endings, I close the course with Robert Mason's *Weapon*. Mason is the author of an excellent memoir of helicopter warfare called *Chickenhawk*, but if I used that, I'd have to drop

Close Quarters. Moreover, *Weapon* does something I can't do with *Chickenhawk.* Set in Nicaragua in 1988, *Weapon* allows me to pull the entire Vietnam experience out of history and connect it to the world we live in today. There is little value to history if one cannot demonstrate its relevance to the present and the future, and that's what *Weapon* does.

That's the course, in a nutshell. It begins, as the war did, forty years ago; it ends in the present, just as the war and its aftermath have stayed with us. My students and I have also had the added advantage of classroom visits by Jan Barry, Larry Heinemann, Yusef Komunyakaa, and David V. Connolly, a Vietnam veteran and poet from South Boston. But you don't have to be a student to take this course. You can read all of these books on your own and come away with a pretty decent understanding of a very complex and unsettling time.

Certainly, the course does not cover every aspect of the war. I would like to have spent more time on the experience of black soldiers, and had intended to use A. R. Flowers's novel *De Mojo Blues,* but the book is out of print, so the only black voices the students hear are Coleman's and Komunyakaa's. I would like to have had more literature by Vietnamese; after all, it was their country. The voices of support troops and rear echelon soldiers, ten times more numerous than actual combat troops, go unheard, though had time permitted, I might have used John Ketwig's memoir *And a Hard Rain Fell* or David A. Willson's novel *REMF Diary.* If there is a good work of literature dealing with Cambodia, I am not familiar with it, and Asa Baber's novel of Laos, *Land of a Million Elephants,* has been out of print for twenty years.

I could go on almost indefinitely about what is missing from my course, but no single course could ever begin to cover it all. What I have tried to do is to offer as broad a range of material and voices as possible in the time available to me. For students who seldom read, except when they are required to, it is invariably a revelation, often a difficult and uncomfortable revelation.

But that's okay. In fact, that's the whole point. I want them to imagine, however imperfectly, the dilemma of a boy with a fresh draft notice in his hand, the weight of a rucksack after ten hours of humping the boonies, the damage high speed steel does to human flesh, the terrible anguish that is so benignly pigeonholed as Post Traumatic Stress Disorder.

Had U.S. policymakers possessed a little imagination, they might have heeded Graham Greene's warning. Had the American people heard that voice trailing off "as though it were the end of an early-morning party, with wine bottles and beer bottles lined up along the windowsills and across the floor and everybody out of cigarettes," they might have asked a few more questions before allowing their children to be sent halfway around the world to kill and be killed. Human lives, our own or anyone else's, ought not to be squandered. A little imagination might have saved the world a whole lot of trouble. It might still. And there is nothing to stimulate the imagination like a good book.

ON U.S. POLICY TOWARD
POST-WAR VIETNAM

In late 1985, I returned to Vietnam for the first time since I'd fought there as a young Marine in 1967–68. Not surprisingly, I found a people who were still visibly suffering from eighty years of French colonization, thirty years of war, and ten years of international isolation spearheaded by the U.S. government.

But suffering is nothing new to the people of Vietnam, whose 4,000-year history is characterized by almost perpetual struggle against larger outside powers intent upon bending Vietnam to their own ends. What is truly remarkable about Vietnamese history is that none of these outside powers has ever managed to destroy Vietnam or the Vietnamese people's sense of themselves as a distinct culture and nation.

China actually occupied Vietnam for more than a thousand years, only to be expelled decisively in A.D. 938. Since then, three Chinese invasions have been repulsed, along with three Mongol invasions and an invasion by the Siamese. In the 20th century, the French, the Japanese and the Americans have fared no better.

Indeed, the latest "war" against Vietnam, the U.S.-imposed economic and diplomatic embargo now in its sixteenth year, is once again proving the toughness, resourcefulness and resilience of these remarkable people Americans have so consistently misunderstood and underestimated, a fact brought home to me quite forcefully during my second postwar visit to Vietnam in June 1990.

For in spite of the best (or worst) efforts of the U.S. government to punish the people of Vietnam for having the audacity to thwart

149

U.S. aims fifteen years ago, Vietnam and its people have made remarkable progress in the past five years.

In 1985, the trains I saw were pulled by ancient steam locomotives. In 1990, the only steam engine I saw was working a freight siding; most trains are pulled by new diesel engines. In 1985, Vietnam's commercial airline was flying outdated turboprops. In 1990, it has a fleet of jets. In 1985, Vietnam was still importing rice. In 1990, it is again a rice-exporting country for the first time in 30 years.

In 1985, when the sun went down, Vietnam was plunged into darkness. In 1990, electrification is widespread. Hanoi and Ho Chi Minh City are lit by streetlights, and most homes have electric lighting. Even many of the small villages I visited are electrified, and the supply of electricity is vastly more dependable than the little that was available in 1985.

Along with electricity has come television. In 1985, I watched TV only once, in a hotel lobby: a Russian newscast with Vietnamese dubbed in. In 1990, many city-dwellers north and south have television. The whole country seemed to be watching the World Cup. Hanoi alone has four competing stations, and I saw TV aerials even in relatively remote towns and villages.

In 1985, Hanoi still relied on a rickety old French-built trolley system. In 1990, the city is crisscrossed by electric buses. In 1985, motor vehicles were rare, especially in the north. In 1990, the still-ubiquitous bicycles compete with motorscooters, cars, trucks and buses. In 1985, I saw nary a tractor in all of Vietnam. In 1990, though water buffalo and cattle still predominate, I saw half a dozen tractors working fields between Hanoi and Haiphong alone.

Everywhere new housing is going up: modest one- and two-room homes, but all of them made with locally produced concrete, brick and tile. The site of my old battalion command post near Hoi An, where once there was nothing but sand, sandbags and barbed wire, is now a village of several thousand people, all living in small but well-built homes.

It is as if the Americans had never been there, which is especially ironic because everyone else is there *except* the Americans. The Australians have built a luxurious floating hotel on the Saigon River. The Japanese are refurbishing the old Metropole in Hanoi. The British, Dutch, French and Russians are pumping oil from deposits in Vietnamese coastal waters. I traveled the roads of

Vietnam in an air-conditioned Toyota mini-bus. The hotels I stayed in were stocked with soap from Thailand and beer from Holland. Stores and street stalls from Hanoi to Ho Chi Minh City sell Japanese tape decks, German film, Saudi Arabian bottled spring water, shampoo from Malaysia, toys from China and electric fans from Singapore. One can buy Rambo sew-on patches and Playboy belt buckles and even model F-16's made in Taiwan with "U.S. Air Force" stenciled on the sides.

Vietnam has hardly become a prosperous country. For most Vietnamese, life remains hard and unforgiving. Watching men, women and children planting rice shoots by hand under a blistering sun gives new meaning to the term "stoop labor." But they continue to plant their rice as they have done for forty centuries. And all around them is undeniable evidence that life is getting better.

So the joke's on us, really, as it has been all along. The people of Vietnam are not likely to pay any more attention to George Bush than they did to Harry Truman, Dwight Eisenhower, John Kennedy, Lyndon Johnson, Richard Nixon, Gerald Ford, Jimmy Carter or Ronald Reagan.

From the highest official to the lowliest peasant, the people of Vietnam carry their hard but proud history in their bones. They will persevere, as they always have. If they have to do it alone, they will do it alone. If anyone wants to help them, quite obviously they will take whatever help is offered.

Most of the rest of the world has long since begun to offer that help in return for the resources, labor and profits a nation of seventy million people has to offer. It is not a matter of ideology or morality; it is simply dollars and cents, and even our closest allies are turning their backs on the petulant stubbornness of the U.S. government.

On a flight from Hanoi to Danang, I sat next to an English geologist employed by British Petroleum. He found it quite humorous that George Bush, the Texas oilman, is screwing his Texas oil buddies with his shortsighted insistence on continuing an embargo as outmoded as the dinosaurs. "By the time old George comes to his senses," the Englishman laughed, "there'll be no more oil left to pump."

Of course, many U.S. businessmen are more than ready to do business with Vietnam, as evidenced by recent articles in *The Philadelphia Inquirer* and *Newsweek*. But the U.S. government remains stuck in a time warp, unable to escape the humbling past and accept the reality of Vietnam in the 1990's.

Twenty years ago, during the war, most of the rest of the world thought the U.S. government was crazy to be doing what it was doing to Vietnam. A lot of things have changed since then, but the U.S. government is still pursuing a dead-end and counterproductive policy, and the rest of the world is still shaking its collective head in wonder. Meanwhile, the people of Vietnam go about their lives with energy and patience and pride. A culture that was already three thousand years old when William of Normandy conquered Saxon England knows a thing or two about survival.

DON'T STAND ON PROTOCOL

He is a small man, five feet-four inches, perhaps five-five, slightly built and radiating vitality, though his hair is silver-gray, the hairline deeply receded. As he enters the elegant hall in Hanoi where I've been waiting, I stand immediately, coming almost to attention as if by instinct, but he gestures casually for me to sit down again. "Don't stand on protocol," he says through a translator. "I was once a teacher and a writer—like you. I still write poems occasionally, so this is a meeting of colleagues.

"The last time you [Americans] came here," he continues, "circumstances were different. Back then, you were always up in the sky, and we had to listen for air raids. I think today we will not have to run for the bomb shelters." He laughs comfortably, enjoying his own joke, his face crinkling into a warm, almost elfin smile.

His easy graciousness is disarming, but in spite of his assurances, this is hardly a meeting of colleagues. Though his plain green uniform bears neither medals nor ribbons—no adornments save two red collar tabs and two yellow shoulderboards, each with four gold stars—this man was already a living legend when I was fighting in Vietnam as a young enlisted Marine twenty-three years earlier. This man is one of the great generals of the 20th century, and perhaps of all time. This man is Vo Nguyen Giap.

Giap, born in 1912 in the village of An Xa just north of the 17th parallel, had indeed been a history teacher and a journalist as a young man. But in 1944, Ho Chi Minh asked Giap to build an army for him. Ten years later, the army Giap built and led defeated the French at what French writer Bernard Fall appropriately called "hell in a very small place": Dien Bien Phu. The impossible

153

campaign Giap waged with superb strategy, superior tactics, unimaginable human effort and sheer determination is still studied in military colleges all over the world.

In that isolated valley near the Laotian border, 15,000 French colonial soldiers—many of them elite Foreign Legion and parachute battalions—dared Giap to take them on, never dreaming he could begin to muster the resources to accept their challenge. It took Giap three months, but he managed to bring in 50,000 of his own soldiers and over 200 heavy guns—the guns hauled much of the way through mountainous jungle by human muscle alone, half a mile a day—and in the end, Giap won. He was then exactly the same age I am now.

Giap's victory at Dien Bien Phu marked an ignominious end to French colonial rule in Indochina. It should also have meant independence for all of Vietnam, but it didn't. "After the Geneva Accords were signed in 1954," Giap says, "we tried to abide by them and reunite Vietnam by peaceful means. But the U.S. and Ngo Dinh Diem [the American-sponsored ruler of southern Vietnam] wouldn't permit that, so we had to fight again." Constantly and deftly changing tactics to match changing military and political circumstances, he won that war, too, a victory perhaps even more astounding than his defeat of the French.

In early January 1968, as I patrolled the rolling hills south of Quang Tri searching for Giap's army, U.S. attention was increasingly directed toward an isolated outpost northwest of us called Khe Sanh. There, my brother Marines were dug in awaiting an anticipated North Vietnamese assault that everyone from the politicians to the journalists was likening to Dien Bien Phu. William Westmoreland, the commanding general of U.S. forces in Vietnam, was convinced that Giap was going to try to duplicate his decisive 1954 battle. He kept talking about some sort of light at the end of some tunnel. Instead, Giap unleashed the Tet Offensive, catching all of us completely unprepared, and Giap's army nearly killed me in the streets of Hue.

"Eat," he says, peeling and handing me a fresh lichee nut as he talks. "The Americans were too proud. You had material strength on your side, but we had the people. In such a struggle, the people will win every time." In 1975, Giap explains, when the long war was finally over, the first place he went to in Saigon (which was immediately renamed Ho Chi Minh City) was the headquarters of the defeated South Vietnamese General Staff. "They had every modern weapon—lasers, electronics, artillery, aircraft—and we didn't. But we won anyway. They couldn't defeat the people."

When I ask Giap what he might have done differently, had he been a U.S. general, he replies, "If I had been an American general, I would not have fought in Vietnam." Again that radiant smile. Then he gestures around the room we are in, explaining that this was once the French governor general's mansion. "The French, the Japanese, the Chinese, the Americans. I've seen them all come and go. All we have ever wanted is peace, freedom and independence. We have never wanted war, but we have never accepted slavery to any foreign invaders."

Giap looks and sounds more like a school teacher than a soldier. His voice conveys humor, wit, and even kindness. It is easier to imagine him coaxing a nervous student through a recitation than sending young men and even women to certain death in battle. But his sparkling eyes are as keen as razors; they crackle with intelligence and strength. One can still feel the heat of the fire burning within him, and as he talks, one begins to understand the source of that fire.

"Vietnam is one nation," Giap says. "Love for one's country means love for one's people. Ho Chi Minh understood that. I am very sorry that you cannot meet him; you would see that he was a human being just like yourself. But I would have been a revolutionary even if I had never met him. I have always been a resistance fighter. I come from a peasant family. My father was heavily taxed by the landlord. And when my mother hired the boat to transport the rice to pay the landlord, she had to pay the landlord for using the boat. I was there in the boat. I saw everything. When I was young, Vietnam was a lost country."

Involved in anti-colonial agitation by the age of 14, at 18 Giap was jailed for three years by the French. At age 24, after organizing a national student strike against the French, he went underground. When he was 31, his first wife died in prison while serving a life sentence for "conspiracy." Soon after, in the midst of the Japanese occupation of Vietnam at the height of the Second World War, Giap joined with Ho Chi Minh and Pham Van Dong to form the Viet Minh, which became the political and military voice of Vietnamese national aspirations.

It is a great irony of history that in those days he and his small

Viet Minh force were being trained, equipped and assisted by a team of American soldiers from the Office of Strategic Services (forerunner of the C.I.A.). In return, the Viet Minh rescued downed U.S. pilots and provided the Americans with vital intelligence on the Japanese. On September 2, 1945, more than a year before the First Indochina War with the French even began, the O.S.S. team leader, Major Archimedes Patti, stood next to Giap on the reviewing stand in Hanoi while Ho Chi Minh declared Vietnam an independent nation. Patti believed the United States should recognize and assist the new nation, but policymakers in Washington, D.C., paid him no heed. Had those distant men listened to their own lieutenant, Giap might have gone back to teaching, and millions of lives might have been spared.

But we as a people and a nation have always misjudged, misunderstood and underestimated the Vietnamese, and that is no less true today than it was 45 years ago. The U.S. still maintains a diplomatic and economic embargo against Vietnam, fifteen years after the end of the war. Giap would like to see a normalization of relations between the U.S. and Vietnam. "We have a duty toward mutual understanding," he says. Citing Article 21 of the 1973 Paris Accords, which deals with war reparations, he argues that the U.S. is "still morally obligated to Vietnam." He mentions French, Japanese and Australian investment in Vietnam, then says that he would like to see U.S. investment as well.

In spite of U.S. obstinacy, however, Giap believes that Vietnam will eventually prevail. "Hardships still exist," he says, "but things are getting better. There are two- and even three-story houses now in villages that were once nothing but straw and bamboo. In my first battle, I had one grenade. When I threw it, it didn't explode. At Dien Bien Phu, the obstacles we faced were insurmountable, but we prevailed. All Vietnamese, whether communist or not, are patriots. Certainly we have difficulties today, but we are optimistic. That's what the Vietnamese people are."

"I expect you get very tired of answering questions about the war," I ask near the end of our time together. "When you don't have to meet with people like me, boring things like this, what do you like to do with your time now?"

"I like to play Vietnamese musical instruments as well as play the piano," Giap replies almost merrily, his face suddenly beaming.

"When we play the piano, our hands must move, our eyes must look, our ears must listen—and then the mind is free."

As I listen to Giap speak, watching his hands move as if playing an invisible piano, his eyes alive with energy and fire, I am reminded of the oft-repeated words of my former commander-in-chief in Vietnam: "Throughout the war, we never lost a battle. We had some companies that were badly hurt . . . but we did not lose a battle of consequence." Here in Hanoi, in the sweltering heat of a June afternoon fifteen years after the end of the war the Americans didn't win, the hollowness of those words rings in the air like bats' wings flapping in a belfry. Sitting across from me is a small, determined man who indeed lost many battles over the course of his long lifetime. But General Vo Nguyen Giap never lost a war.

HUE CITY RE-VISITED

January 31, 1968, was the most violent day of my life. Our battalion had just come down to Phu Bai after four months up around the Demilitarized Zone. That morning before dawn, the U.S. Army MACV compound in Hue City had radioed down to Phu Bai that they were taking incoming small arms and light mortar fire. So we'd saddled up a small relief column of Marines, loaded onto trucks, and headed up Highway One toward Hue to check it out.

I was nineteen years old. I'd been in Vietnam almost a year to the day, and I thought I'd seen everything, but I'd never seen anything like what was about to happen. What we drove into, as we approached the south edge of the city, was a murderously perfect ambush that struck with the force of a steel hurricane. Viet Cong and North Vietnamese soldiers opened up on our convoy from concealed positions at point blank range with AK-47s, mortars, rockets, recoilless rifles and heavy machineguns. They were dug in on either side of the street, in the buildings, behind walls, on rooftops.

We neither knew nor cared at the time that this was the beginning of what would later come to be known as the Tet Offensive of 1968. We were only trying to survive. It took us fourteen hours and heavy casualties to fight our way seven blocks to the MACV compound, and the next several weeks were just as ugly: house-to-house streetfighting against a well-trained, well-equipped adversary who initially had us heavily outnumbered and was determined to hold the city for as long as possible.

Six days after that first ambush, I was wounded by shrapnel from a B-40 rocket. I lost my hearing completely for several weeks, and a few holes needed to be plugged up, but I kept fighting. It wasn't heroism. The rule of the moment was: if you can see, walk and shoot, you stay in the line. And so I stayed.

Then one day in the middle of a firefight, my lieutenant had driven up in a jeep, shouting, "Let's go, Ehrhart, your orders are in. There's a chopper on the LZ right now." Ten minutes later, as the helicopter lifted off the landing zone and the fighting fell away beneath me, I thought I was saying goodbye to Hue City and Vietnam forever. And I wasn't sorry to go.

Yet here I am, twenty-two years later, riding up Highway One from Phu Bai, headed for Hue City once again. It is June 19, 1990. I am forty-one years old. As the bus I'm riding in gets closer to Hue, my heart begins to pound and my palms are sweating. What will it be like? How will I react? Will the memory of those terrible days be more than I can handle? There is only one way to find out. As we approach the place we had been ambushed that long ago morning, I ask the driver to stop, and I get out. I am going to walk up that long street into the city, alone, unarmed, all the way to the River of Perfumes.

But it's as if I've stepped into a dream. Everything is at once familiar and strange. There's the canal. There's the big Cathedral, but it's standing all alone much farther from the river than I remember. I begin walking. It's nearly noon, and blistering hot beneath a clear, blue sky. Dust kicks up from the street and turns to thin mud between my toes. I'm not absolutely certain I'm even in the right place.

But I must be. There's the old Shell gas station we'd passed that first morning. I can still see the Shell logo on the three pumps. And just beyond that is the two-story building surrounded by a low concrete wall, in the courtyard of which I had killed an NVA soldier. His body had lain there for nearly a week, until it was decayed and bloated almost beyond recognition and we had finally covered it with earth because we could no longer stand the stench.

But the dreamlike feeling persists. I remember a street lined with multi-story buildings from which we were being fired down on, but for several blocks there is nothing but one-story homes with storefronts. I remember the street being wider and with sidewalks. Am I in the wrong place, or were those buildings destroyed and never replaced? I begin walking faster, peering into bicycle repair shops and butcher shops and shops selling beer, soda, cigarettes and Kodak film.

Twenty-two years ago, the city had seemed deserted. The streets had been empty, the shops closed. Anything that moved was shot at. The only civilians I had seen were the refugees who had taken shelter in the university, and the corpses. Years later, accusations linger that the communists massacred 5,000 unarmed civilians during their occupation of Hue, but many of those who died were undoubtedly nothing more sinister than accidental casualties of the fiercest fighting of the war.

Now there are people everywhere: in the shops, along the street, passing on bicycles and motorbikes. Some people ignore me. Others peer furtively. Still others stare. Westerners are still uncommon here. A few children point and say, "Lien Xo" (Russian). When I shake my head and say, "No Lien Xo. My" (American), they giggle and turn away and look back and giggle again. They chatter at me and each other in their beautiful sing-song language, and I don't know what they are saying, but they seem to find me amusing. At no time do I feel at all threatened.

It occurs to me that I ought to be feeling—what? Where are the flashbacks? The involuntary cringing at open windows? The screams of the wounded carrying down the years? I have become so caught up in this memory puzzle, trying to close the disparity between what I'm seeing and what I remember, that I have hardly thought about the violence except as a kind of abstract, historical artifact. I had fully expected to be afraid, perhaps to shake as if left too long in the cold, or to break down in the street and cry uncontrollably.

Yet all I feel is a euphoric sense of elation. My heart is still racing, but I feel light as a feather. I feel happy, as if I've been given a momentary chance to be 19 again, to walk this street like any ordinary teenager loose in the big city. That first time must have been some sort of bizarre mistake. I wasn't supposed to have come here armed to the teeth, scared to death, and fighting as though there would never be anything else in my life except fighting.

I find the building we had used as our battalion command post, the building I had been in when I was wounded. At least I think it is, but the wall around it is different then I remember, and the entrance is different. Where is the old MACV compound? It should be right across the street, but what looks like the old MACV compound is a full block closer to the river than I remember. Again the momentary confusion, the dreamlike unreality.

But there's the old post office. And there's the easternmost bridge across the River of Perfumes. And the university. And the grassy space between the river and the university that we had used as an LZ. But the university has three buildings, not the single building I remember. And the old LZ is studded with large rocks that have clearly been there for a very long time, though I have no recollection of them.

I traverse several side streets, trying to nail down the loose ends. There's what used to be the Catholic girls' convent school. And there! That's the building from which the NVA gunner with the B-40 had fired at me. I'd been firing from that second-story window over there, just across the street. Wally and Hoffy had actually seen the guy fire. The rocket had entered the window and blown up on the wall four feet above and behind me.

And it all falls into place. I was right from the moment I had stepped off the bus. Of course memory has not been perfect. It was a long time ago, and I had been very young and very frightened, and the fighting had been ferocious. Moreover, any neighborhood changes with time, especially if it's taken the beating this one had.

The building I'd been in when I'd gotten hit had been an elegant place, obviously the home of someone very rich. Now it looks almost derelict, its windows shuttered closed, its yard neglected. Part of the elegant outer wall has been replaced by cinderblocks. I enter the yard to take a closer look, but a young man comes out of the building and shoos me away. I try to explain who I am and why I am here, but he speaks no English and I speak no Vietnamese. It might be his home, for all I know. I apologize and leave. He waves pleasantly as I go.

That night, I cross the river by the same bridge we had crossed that first day of the battle after fighting our way into the city. We had been met on the north bank by the same withering fire we had just fought our way through, losing two quad-.50 caliber machine-gun trucks in a matter of minutes, and had had to fall back almost immediately. A few days later, during the night actually, Viet Cong frogmen had blown the center span of the bridge. It has since been rebuilt, but the cantilever superstructure has never been replaced. The bridge looks vaguely like a grinning mouth with a tooth missing.

At night, it is eerily dark and quiet. The bridge has no lighting of its own, and most of the traffic consists of bicycles and motor-scooters; cars and trucks use the heavier, newer bridge farther west. All along the pedestrian walkway, people stand or sit alone or in small groups, talking or quietly watching the water as if this bridge were their own back porch, which in a way it is. Many of the people are young couples holding hands, and I think to myself what a wonderful spot this is to go courting.

I walk the north bank of the river as far west as the famous Citadel, home of the last imperial dynasty, the last piece of real estate reluctantly relinquished by the VC and NVA during the Tet Offensive. Along the way, I pass several riverside nightclubs from which the sounds of young laughter and rock-and-roll music float out over the dark water. I cross the street and start back. This side of the street is packed with homes and shops and sidewalk cafes, a movie house, a rollerskating rink, sidewalk vendors, pedestrians and bicycles, whole families eating supper on their doorsteps, small cooking fires set up right on the sidewalk.

I pass two small girls playing badminton on the sidewalk without a net, and soon I am part of the game. I can hardly see the birdie in the darkness, but the girls don't seem to mind, and soon a whole crowd has gathered to watch. When the girls' mother appears, I pull out a picture of my own wife and daughter, hoping to convince her that this strange westerner can be trusted. Soon she offers me a stool, calls to her husband, and they both sit down with me. Then another daughter appears, then a son and a nephew. The boys, young men really, ages 22 and 23, speak a little English and are eager to practice.

We start with names. Mine in Vietnamese is rendered "E-hat." My daughter is "Li-la," my wife "Anh." The mother and father are Suong and Nga, their children are Tung, Tra My, Diem My and Diem Chau. The nephew is Hiep. Tung is a medical student, Hiep a recent college graduate who will begin teaching high school in September. The girls, ages 14, 11 and 8, are all in school.

They want to know why I'm here. I tell them that I am a writer, that when I was a young man, I had been an American Marine and had fought here during Tet 1968. I point across the river, and gesture as if I were aiming a shoulder-fired rocket, show them my scars, and say "VC." Only then does Mr. Nga, who is 48, tell me that he had once been a South Vietnamese army lieutenant who was captured by the North Vietnamese in 1971 and held as a prisoner of war for six years. Now he runs this small retail shop, in front of which we are sitting.

I ask him what he thinks of the new regime. He just shrugs. "It's better than war," he says finally. Then he adds that he has a sister in California, and his wife has a brother in Texas. They would like to go to the U.S., too, but it costs a lot of money. He does not think they will ever be able to go.

Turning to Tung, I say, "Your father fought for the Saigon regime, but you are going to medical school. How did that happen?" Tung explains that he took a competitive examination, and scored well; what his father did during the war has not been held against him. I ask him what he would do if his parents and sisters ever did go to the U.S. "Oh, I would go, too," he says with a grin. "I would like to be a doctor in America."

"Do you want to go to America, too?" I ask Hiep.

"No," says Hiep. "This is my country. I will stay here."

The next day, I am introduced to the People's Committee of Thua Thien Province. During our conversation, I explain to them where I was wounded and ask them if they know what that building is used for now. No one seems to know, but a man named Nguyen Dac Xuan asks me if I would like to find out. He motions for me to follow him, and we walk right out of the meeting, get on his Honda motorscooter, and drive the few blocks right then and there. He knocks on the door, and the same man who had waved me off the day before answers.

There is a conversation in Vietnamese, then Mr. Xuan tells me that this was once a South Vietnamese army general's home, but is now an Army Guest House. The other man is the caretaker. He has told Mr. Xuan that he remembers me from the day before, that he is sorry he had to ask me to leave, but he did not know who I was and was only doing his job. I thank the caretaker, and we walk up to the river, talking as we go.

"We might have killed one another back then," Mr. Xuan says softly, taking my arm. "I fought here, too, during the General Uprising" (which is what the Vietnamese call the Tet Offensive). He is 53 years old, he tells me, a native of Hue, and a writer like myself. During his student days at the university, he became involved in the anti-war movement. At that time, he was not a communist, but he was openly opposed to the Saigon regime, and his anti-war activities attracted the unwelcome attention of the government. In 1966, he got word from a friend that he was about to be arrested, so he fled west to the jungle.

From then until the end of the war, he operated locally with Viet Cong forces as a military journalist, though he did not join the communist party until 1973. During the Tet Offensive, he had guided North Vietnamese troops into the Citadel. There he had had to abandon his official job because of the heavy fighting; instead he had helped tend the wounded and bury the dead. "There was no time for writing," he says. "We were fighting for our lives." He pauses before adding, "You know what I'm talking about, don't you?"

I ask him about the so-called "Hue massacre," mentioning the figure of 5,000 commonly cited in the U.S. He stares at me in disbelief. "Not five thousand," he says. "You were here. You saw what happened. People could not protect themselves, and they got killed." Then he tells me that several hundred people were arrested in the early days of the fighting, but that all of them had had direct ties to the "puppet regime," by which he means the old Saigon government. They were to have been taken west to the mountain strongholds, but the Americans closed the escape routes faster than the VC had anticipated. Cut off and unable to obtain new orders, the guards chose to kill their prisoners and escape individually or in small groups. "Perhaps they should not have killed those people," he says. "But consider what the French did to those who collaborated with the Nazis. What's the difference? Would you be willing to die trying to save traitors?"

That night, Mr. Xuan and my other hosts take me down to the river where a sampan is waiting. On board are five musicians and five young singers dressed in *ao dais*, the graceful traditional dresses worn by Vietnamese women. The sun is down by the time we cast off, and the boatman heads west upriver, using the engine for awhile, then working only with a long oar.

For the next three hours, we drift slowly on the dark river flanked by the two halves of the darkened city while the musicians and singers transport us back to a world and a culture that have been here in this place for centuries. Between songs, we recite poems to each other in Vietnamese and English, sip hot tea, and listen to the water gently slapping the hull only inches from our heads. Once more, I feel like I'm in a dream, but this dream is soft and soothing and magical.

As we drift under the bridge, I think back to the night the vc blew it up. I had stood on the south bank of the river that night, staring at the broken bridge and the black water, knowing the river was as hostile as the city on either side of it. One of the women is singing without accompaniment, her voice like lapping water, and I let her words wash over me, cleansing me of the terrible memories I have carried all these years. "If there were peace, this river would be a peaceful place," poet and Vietnam veteran John Balaban wrote years ago about the River of Perfumes. Now there is peace, and this river is indeed a peaceful place.

A COMMON LANGUAGE

"Writers are the engineers of the soul."
General Tran Van Tra
Ho Chi Minh City
June 24, 1990

"I was born in 1949," Le Minh Khue began quietly. "That is to say I'm one year younger than W. D. Ehrhart. In wartime, he served with a rifle in the U.S. Marines, fought in Hue, a poetic city of my country. As for me, I was then on Roads 15 and 20, not far from Hue, on a section of the famous Ho Chi Minh Trail, as a member of a young volunteers' team under the military engineering command. I never saw an American soldier in battledress. If I had met you then in your Marine 'utes,' maybe I'd be scared to death, and this fear would remain with me all my life."

Though Khue was nominally addressing her remarks to the entire nine-member U.S. delegation assembled at Hanoi's West Lake Guest House for this first-ever Conference of U.S. and Vietnamese Veteran-Writers, she was looking directly at me; I was the one who the previous day had referred to "utes" (utilities: what the U.S. Army called fatigues). I adjusted my headset, from which the simultaneous English translation was coming, and listened intently, startled and curious.

"Today I meet you here, as a writer, a poet," she continued. "We talk and find out we both have memories of the war, we both have spent our youth in the same fierce space, though on opposite sides. I've heard you reciting your poems, your friends speaking about my country in amiable words, and I'm extremely moved by the thought that human beings can be kind and open-hearted to their

166

fellow human beings. I'd like to speak a little about myself, so that you can understand how soldiers of my generation — some of them are present here today — became writers.

"The day I went to the front, I left my family, my parents, brothers and sisters, this sweet home of mine shaken by the turmoil of war. My comrades and I were then students who quit high school to join in the heroic atmosphere of the moment. We had, of course, many books in our knapsacks. The ones I brought with me were by Ernest Hemingway and Jack London, two authors whose novels and short stories had been translated into Vietnamese and were much prized by my parents. In those days, there were many things that helped us to overcome trials and difficulties: our comradeship in arms, our confidence in the future. But there were two men who gave me much more assistance: Hemingway and London. I loved them and shall love them forever.

"We worked then at a crucial place on the north-south supply line. We were many times the targets of U.S. Air Force bombing. I never fired one shot, but my comrades and I defused delayed-action bombs. We were subjected to acid showers produced by thousands and thousands of silver iodine crystals dropped into the clouds. We struggled against incendiaries, mines, bombs and other killing devices. We endured many privations almost too horrible to speak of.

"In those hard days, I read over and over again these two American authors. I learned a love of life from Jack London, as well as the courage to transcend death, to keep up hope against any odds. I liked very much the tough men in London's stories who fought blizzard and death for survival. I cherished the anguish of Hemingway, whose wonderful short stories deal with loneliness, death, and love of life, eternal topics of literature and human thought. And my love of literature stems from these two and from that time.

"My friends fought with great courage to keep the road open to traffic, and I began to write about them. Many of them died at the age of eighteen. Others survived the war, but have lost their youth. How you returned to normal life, I don't know, but you write poems. I prefer short stories, but just like you, I worry about the future of humanity. We have to get rid of the aftermath of war inside each of us. We have to struggle against disinterest in the face of others' suffering, against greed and the baseness that corrodes heart and mind. We must teach each other to love, so that war will never, never happen again."

When I left Vietnam on January 2, 1986, having spent most of December 1985 there, it never occurred to me that I would ever come back. It had been a long trip, an expensive trip, a difficult trip emotionally, a once-in-a-lifetime journey. In the 18 years since I'd left Vietnam as a 19-year-old battle-weary Marine, no matter how hard I'd tried, I had never been able to see in my mind's eye a Vietnam other than the one then in the midst of war. And all my memories were in black and white. I had wanted to see Vietnam at peace. I had wanted to see Vietnam in color. I had wanted to see once more this faraway land that had become, with the passing years, more a state of mind than a geographical location, to give it and its people substance and place and breath. And I had done that in 1985. The circle had been closed. I could finally move on.

But Vietnam has insinuated itself into my life in ways both large and small to a degree I never imagined possible even five years ago. For better or worse, I have become identified as a "Vietnam writer" and a sort of spokesperson for the American experience in Vietnam. While I dislike the label (and would rather not have had the experience), it has brought me opportunities I would never otherwise have had, among them two trips to Britain, a lecture tour of Austria, Germany and Yugoslavia, and in January 1990 a semester's appointment as Visiting Professor at the William Joiner Center for the Study of War and Social Consequences at the University of Massachusetts at Boston. Like it or not, Vietnam is now a permanent fact of my life.

So when the Joiner Center began working with the Writers' Association of Vietnam to bring together this conference, and asked me if I was interested in participating, I figured, "Sure, why not?" After all, Vietnam is a fascinating place, as most foreign lands are. And it would be an honor to be part of the first official U.S. writers' delegation to Vietnam. And besides, in 1985 I had seen only Hanoi and Ho Chi Minh City. I had not gotten to see any of the places in central Vietnam where I had lived and fought. I had told myself then that it didn't really matter, but it had. This time, I could really close the circle.

The idea for the conference grew out of a 1989 visit to the Joiner Center's annual Veteran Writers' Workshop by Nguyen Quang

Sang and Nguyen Khai, deputy secretary general and executive member of the Vietnam Writers' Association respectively, and Le Luu, currently Vietnam's most popular living novelist. The three men had been given a very rough time by extremist right-wing elements of the Vietnamese immigrant community here in the U.S. After one public event, during a well-orchestrated "demonstration" in front of the Boston Public Library, they and their American companions were physically assaulted by hysterical Vietnamese emigres, many of them too young to have anything but the vaguest memories of the land in which they were born. I came away from that night with two thoughts: Where was all this Vietnamese freedom-loving piss-and-vinegar when I was slogging through the ricefields in 1967? And: If these three guys ever get back to Vietnam alive, they ain't ever gonna wanna see any of us again.

I'm still wondering about that first thought, but apparently my second thought was wrong. However shaken they may have been, Sang, Khai and Le Luu were not deterred, and nine months later, on June 13 and 14, 1990, the conference was held on the grounds of the complex where the Politburo used to take shelter during the worst of the U.S. bombing. The Vietnamese were represented by 31 writers and poets along with several dozen unofficial delegates and observers. The American delegation consisted of, in addition to myself, Philip Caputo (*A Rumor of War*), Larry Heinemann (*Close Quarters*), Yusef Komunyakaa (*Dien Cai Dau*), Larry Rottmann (*American Eagle*), Bruce Weigl (*Song of Napalm*), *Washington Post* reporter George Wilson, and Joiner Center co-directors Kevin Bowen and David Hunt.

Vu Tu Nam, Writers' Association general secretary, opened the conference by telling us that we would meet "open-hearted men, gentle women and unassuming war veterans who were once designated by the U.S. armed forces under the common name of Viet Cong; we can assure you that wherever you go, you'll be welcomed by hospitable smiles." This, it turned out, would be largely true, but there *had* been Viet Cong in Vietnam, and they *had* tried to kill me. I spent most of that first day and part of the next wondering who in Vietnam had actually done the fighting.

Khue said she hadn't fired a shot or seen a U.S. soldier. Poet Pham Tien Duat, 49, told us: "I spent thirteen years in the army, mostly in the north and along the Ho Chi Minh Trail. I fired only twelve shots, and I hit no one, but the Americans still tried to kill

I

me." Added Xuan Thieu, 60, who also never saw a U.S. soldier: "You didn't see the enemy, but suddenly the messengers of death came for you." By mid-morning of the second day, I began to wonder if these folks weren't pulling their punches.

Then novelist Cao Tien Le stood up. He gestured around the room at his colleagues. "I don't understand all this talk about not shooting Americans," he began, his voice hard at the edges. His eyes bored straight into the Americans sitting across from him. "I killed Americans—the equivalent of a whole platoon. It was my duty, my profession. I was very good at it." The passion in his voice required no translation. His words snapped like rifle shots. "When I was stationed near Khe Sanh on Route 9, we thought it was very funny of the Americans to transport shower water. We used to look for the showers, and shoot the Marines when they took their showers.

"Now things are different, so I won't shoot you," the 51-year-old former infantry company commander managed to add with something like a smile, though I had the feeling at that moment that he would have liked to, even now, fifteen years after the war had finally ended. And why not? We had come half a world to wage war on him and his people. We had unleashed upon the very city in which we were now meeting the most massive aerial bombardment in history. We had spent nearly thirty years struggling mightily to keep Vietnam from its own destiny, and when we failed, like petulant children, we embarked upon an economic and diplomatic war that is still underway.

I had been deeply touched by the warmth of Le Minh Khue, by the irony of her carrying Hemingway and London into the war against the Americans (a phenomenon which many other Vietnamese writers were to confirm over the next few weeks). The atmosphere of cordiality that had prevailed for the first day and a half had been delightful, even uplifting—but it had also seemed a bit unreal, as though these people were politely ignoring who had been responsible for their misery. Cao Tien Le was a dose of reality, unsettling but oddly reassuring.

"I'll tell you what I dream about," Le continued. "Once on the trail we were bombed by B-52s. A lot of soldiers were killed, buried in the earth. But some of the dead still had arms or legs or heads sticking out. More troops were coming down the trail behind us.

We didn't have time to bury the dead properly, and we didn't want the other troops to see them because it was too disturbing. So we had to cut off the protruding limbs, even the heads, of the dead soldiers." As Le talked, former Marine lieutenant Caputo leaned over and whispered, "We could have used him in the Marines."

But even Le was not as fiercely belligerent as he seemed, and perhaps wanted to seem to us. "Once I slept in the same shelter with some captured Americans," he said. "We were all listening to American Armed Forces Radio, and the Americans were singing along with the songs. I realized then that they were human like us — but I couldn't allow myself to think about that. Not then. Now I work in the Youth Publishing House. I want younger generations to understand how terrible war is. I want them to have peace."

Le's apparently impromptu outburst seemed to strike a chord with the Americans, and with the other Vietnamese as well. "Many of my friends were burned to death," responded Heinemann, driver of an armored personnel carrier during the war. "Their remains were no bigger than a roast chicken. Writing about the war will always be obscene because war is obscene. There's no other way to write about it." Added Caputo, "War is a kind of hideous laboratory for studying human nature." And Komunyakaa told the Vietnamese that the war had so troubled him, it was fourteen years before he could begin to write about it.

Huu Thinh, 48, who rose from private to lieutenant colonel during the war, spoke of his own family as a microcosm of the war: one brother killed, one brother permanently brain-damaged and institutionalized. "I am the lucky son. I survived unharmed. But those of us who survived have a debt to pay to those who didn't. Our writing must be responsible. We must see that this never happens again."

"Holding a pen is one thousand times more difficult than holding a rifle," added Khuat Quang Thuy, who joined the army at 17 in 1967 and fought in the south, "for when you hold a rifle, you can easily open fire on order, but when you hold a pen, you can only write in answer to the call of your heart, of your conscience. It is for that reason, I think, that you Americans have found your way back to this country, and that this wonderful meeting has materialized."

"My heart is filled with emotion," said poet Nguyen Thi Ngoc

Tu, 47, "as I come to this extraordinary meeting between represen-
tatives of the two hostile forces in a historic war that lasted nearly
a quarter of a century, half a human life, and in many cases the
whole life of those young people who fell on the battlefields, from
your side as well as ours. But I am rather perplexed, I dare say, by
the small attendance of women veteran-writers at this conference.
[Tu and Khue were the only women delegates from either side.] I
don't know whether there are any women veterans in the United
States, but in our country they make up a considerable number.

"As I attend this meeting, I recall with deep sorrow a friend of
mine, a woman writer who died in the war. She was a native of
Hanoi. In 1967, she was still very young, and was leading a happy
life beside her husband and their lovely year-old daughter. But her
husband was called to the front, and soon thereafter she, too, had
to part with her little daughter and her old mother in answer to the
urgent call of the Motherland.

"She once related to me the scene of her parting. It was evening
when she and her child arrived at the village where her mother had
been evacuated to. The whole night she did not sleep a wink,
spending her time instead counting down the minutes she had left
with her baby, wondering when she would see her child again. 'By
that time, she may have grown into a young girl and entered the
university,' she thought. But the thought was fleeting. Who would
survive this increasingly fierce war? At daybreak she got up, said a
few words of comfort to her mother, kissed the baby, and quietly
left without waking her.

"'Why didn't you wake her up?' I asked her.

"'I could not bear to hear her crying and begging me to take her
with me,' my friend replied, the tears running down her cheeks.

"The image of that toddling baby learning to walk was at once
my friend's sorrow and comfort. Then one enemy bullet knocked
her down, leaving behind the unfinished pages of her book. Whose
bullet? Did it come from any of you here?

"The great dream of us women is to be allowed to live a peaceful,
safe, and happy life with our husbands and children. But as a Vietnamese saying goes, 'When the enemy comes, the women fight,
too.' So many mothers had to part with their children, so many
wives had to part with their husbands, Vietnamese and American.
How many women have become widows in their prime and lonely
in their old age? There were mothers in southern Vietnam who

sheltered liberation fighters, young girls on the front who worked as food and ammunition suppliers, as nurses carrying wounded soldiers, women who shot down enemy planes or ensured production under rains of bombs and shells.

"In the villages of the north, U.S. bombs rained not only on military targets, as claimed by the White House. All bridges, schools and hospitals in densely populated cities, and at times even peasants working in the fields, were also military targets. Girls were shot dead by U.S. planes while rowing boats taking passengers across rivers; women teachers were killed while standing at their desks giving lessons to their pupils; women doctors were hit by shells while treating patients. During the war years, I chanced to visit villages where the entire male population had gone to the front, leaving only women, children and old folks to continue the work.

"Before coming to Vietnam to take part in the war, you must have led a peaceful life beside your dear ones, your mothers, your wives, sisters and children. You must have imagined the expedition to Vietnam as an exciting trip to a faraway sunny tropical land. But parting must have been painful, and those you left behind must have endured the torments of absence and separation and worry. There must have been untold suffering for the loved ones of those who never returned, or returned in their coffins.

"Time has altered the relationship between us and has brought erstwhile adversaries to the same table. But there are things time will never change: girls lost their youth in waiting, or became widows and spinsters. There were those who, after the first moment of happy reunion, were horribly disillusioned to see their husbands returning from the front with incurable wounds. Dangerous diseases caused by exposure to dioxin—deformed babies, infirmities and a high cancer death rate—are the horrible scourges of women in Vietnam, and I think in the United States as well.

"In the past, these matters were not mentioned in works written about the war. Was it due to the fact that, preoccupied with the urgent demands of revolution and the survival of the nation, we had to devote heart and soul to the cause of victory and put aside our personal griefs and losses? But now that the war is behind us, it is time we spoke of those losses and griefs, for they are the price we paid for today's life.

"I know that in the duffel bags of many American GIs killed in the war, they kept pictures of their girlfriends or wives. How did those women feel when they got back the remains of their loved ones? I long to meet them, those American women, to learn about their sufferings and hopes, ordeals and desperations. I am sure that those women, those soldiers' mothers and wives, whether in Vietnam or the U.S., will one day find some comfort in the deep and boundless sympathy of human beings, whoever they are. Only then can we find a common language, that of love for peace and hatred of war."

"The war is still the most important thing in my poetry," added Pham Tien Duat, who spent ten years on the Ho Chi Minh Trail and is now editor of the journal *Literature and Art.* "I can't get away from it. The poverty of the people has been caused by the war, so when I write about the people's misery, I am really writing about the war." When asked if the war had been a useful experience in terms of his poetry, Duat answered without hesitation: "No."

Of course, the writers with whom we met are those more or less "approved" by the Vietnamese government. All are Writers' Association members in good standing. All were on the winning side. It is impossible to gauge just how much freedom of expression is tolerated these days; doubtless it is far less than what we Americans are accustomed to. But Vietnamese writers are clearly no longer bound, as they were during and immediately after the war, to portray the war as a glorious and unstained struggle, the warriors heroic superbeings. Le Luu's popular 1986 novel, *Thoi Xa Vang,* is the story of a soldier who comes home to an unhappy marriage, adultery, a bitter divorce and emotional emptiness.

Le Luu, 47, joined the North Vietnamese army in 1959, and fought until the end of the war, taking part in the battle for Quang Tri in 1972. The father of two children, he is awaiting promotion to colonel, and is currently the editor of the army literary magazine, one of the most vital and lively literary magazines in the country. "During the war," he said, "we were writing propaganda. We had to use every weapon at our disposal, including our pens, in order to achieve victory. But now we must write about the bitterness and the suffering. I must write honestly now because I don't know how much longer I will live. It is not good for a genuine writer to make governments happy or angry. We are writing for the future, not for the present."

In many ways, the future has already arrived in Vietnam, where a majority of the people are too young to have fought in the war and nearly half the population was not even born when the war ended. After the close of the formal conference, we Americans spent several more days in Hanoi, then drove east to the port city of Haiphong in the comfort of a Toyota minibus to meet with members of the Haiphong Writers' Association. Along the way, we heard the voice of Vietnam's younger generation in the form of Nguyen Quang Thieu, a 32-year-old poet who traveled with us as our interpreter.

A story of Thieu's called "To the Stars" begins with the death of a young man who had aspired to be a poet. His friends want to bury him on the mountaintop, but the village elders refuse permission, saying that he has not lived long enough or accomplished enough to be buried there; only the old and wise and great can be buried close to the stars. So the young people play a series of pranks on the elders, fooling them into thinking that the gods and ghosts are displeased with their decision, and in the end the elders relent and the young man is buried on the mountaintop. Allegorical? "Of course," Thieu replied with a grin.

Then he told us the story of one of his poems: A woman goes to the grave of her son who has been killed in the war and prays to the gods to return the boy safely to her. Instead, the ghosts of her son's comrades appear and tell her that her son is gone, he won't be coming back, and she might as well go home and get on with her life. The poem won first prize from the army literary magazine in 1984, but when Thieu's father, a retired army colonel, read the poem, he was outraged. "That's the future," Thieu replied, whereupon his father slapped Thieu across the face. Thieu left the house, and the two men did not speak for several years, but recently the father asked Thieu to come see him. "I am sorry I slapped you," his father told Thieu. "You were right. The war is over now. What did I fight for if not for you to be able to make the kinds of choices you've made?"

"What about Le Luu?" I asked Thieu. "Where does he fit in?"

"He is a kind of bridge," Thieu replied. "He's part of the generation who fought the war—but he thinks like a young person." And indeed, Le Luu, who also traveled with us through the entire trip, was clearly popular with young and old wherever we went. An infectiously warm and playful man, with a smattering of English picked up during trips to the U.S. in 1988 and 1989, he was affectionate with Thieu yet equally at ease with Vo Nguyen Giap, the most revered living person in Vietnam. That night, a severe electrical storm knocked out the power during our meeting with the Haiphong writers. Shimmering in the glow of hastily lit candles, Le Luu told the gathering, "We were born to love each other, not to kill each other."

We drove back to Hanoi the next day, and from there flew to Danang. This was the airfield I'd flown into as a boy–Marine more than twenty-three years earlier, and from which I'd flown thirteen months later, prematurely old and exhausted both physically and emotionally. Then it was one of the busiest airports in the world. Now it was largely abandoned; row upon row of concrete aircraft revetments, built by the Americans to withstand Viet Cong rocket and mortar attacks, stood empty on either side of the landing strip. Vietnamese air force MIGs periodically took off or landed in flights of two, but otherwise our commercial flight was the only visible activity.

I'd been an "old hand" in Hanoi, having spent nine days there in 1985, but this whole part of the trip was different. This is what I had missed in 1985, and of course, it was this part of Vietnam that held so much of my own past, that had forged me into what I have become. It wasn't fear that I felt as the plane touched down, but a kind of nervous exhilaration, a bit like Christmas morning after a long night of sleepless anticipation: you're pretty sure you've been good enough not to get coal in your stocking, but you're not sure what you *will* get. As we stepped off the plane, Caputo, who had commanded a platoon of Marines just west of Danang in 1965, turned to me and shook my hand. "Welcome to Danang," he said.

Over the next three days, I did my 13-month "tour of duty" in reverse. I'd spent my first eight months in Vietnam twenty miles southeast of Danang, near the city of Hoi An. Then my battalion had shifted north to Quang Tri and the Demilitarized Zone, and finally in early 1968, we'd come back down to Phu Bai just in time to be the first unit sent into Hue City on the first morning of the Tet Offensive.

We left the airport almost immediately, driving north by bus over the spectacular Hai Van Pass toward Hue City. From the top of the pass, where the Annamese Cordillera moves in from the west to cut the coastal plain in two, one can see perhaps forty miles of wildly beautiful coastline: wide white beaches rimming barrier islands broken by rivers meandering down from the mountains through farming and fishing villages and ricefields green with new plantings. One small fishing village perched on a scenic spit of sand at the mouth of a river, and it is not hard to imagine a Club Med sitting on that very spot in the not-too-distant future. Vietnam needs and wants such foreign investment — though the people of that village may be hard-pressed to call it progress.

As we passed a forlorn cluster of abandoned buildings, now nothing but walls without floors or roofs or windows, Le Luu told us that this was all that remains of the once-vast Marine base of Phu Bai. From here to Hue, I would be traveling the same road we'd traveled in the pre-dawn hours of January 31, 1968, oblivious to the fact that we were about to be sucked into the biggest battle of the Vietnam war. When our bus reached the south edge of the city, I asked the driver to stop, and I walked into the city alone, up the same street where I'd fought my way on that first terrible morning of Tet, all the way to the River of Perfumes.

I'd had no idea what to expect this time around, but there were no ghosts waiting for me, and my memory turned out to be pretty solid. I found the building I'd been in when I'd been wounded by shrapnel from a B-40 rocket, and the old MACV compound which had been used variously as our battalion headquarters, first aid station and supply dump, and the university that had become a haven for civilian refugees caught in the fighting. The streets were narrower than I remembered, and full of bustling activity. People noticed me because Westerners are still an unfamiliar sight, but they projected only mild disinterest or friendly curiosity.

When I finally reached our hotel two hours later, David Hunt, with some concern, took me by the arm and asked, "How was it?"

"Fine," I said. I was high as a kite, actually, though I couldn't have explained why, and still can't. That night, on Heinemann's sage advice, I bagged the meeting with the Thua Thien Province Writers' Association and wandered through the city for several hours, still in a state of inexplicable euphoria. I fully expected to awaken at two a.m., crying and shaking and remembering all the noise and fear and confusion and blood that have stayed so vividly in my mind all these years. But it didn't happen. Instead, I awoke the next morning to the realization that whatever might have hurt me in this place was long gone and far away, safely out of reach, just history.

The next morning, we set off by bus for the DMZ. Quang Tri City, a lively place in 1967, was leveled in 1972 and never rebuilt. The airfield I'd watched the Seabees build at a place called Ai Tu in the fall of 1967 is now abandoned, just a level strip of earth with nothing standing. Dong Ha, where we stopped for lunch, is as tawdry as ever, but nothing marks the American presence except the stripped-down hulk of a U.S. tank sitting by a flagpole in the center of town. Farther up the road toward Con Thien, a farmer has built his house next to the hulk of another U.S. tank; the tank is the farmer's pig sty.

We could not get closer than several thousand meters to Con Thien, where I had spent thirty-three days living in the mud while North Vietnamese gunners shelled us with heavy artillery, because the area is still heavily mined and dangerous, but we went all the way to the Ben Hai River, which once marked the boundary between northern and southern Vietnam, where we visited a national cemetery containing the remains of 10,300 Vietnamese who died on the Ho Chi Minh Trail. The rows and rows of low concrete slabs are sobering. Heinemann placed his Army Combat Infantryman's Badge on the grave of a soldier who had been born the same year as himself, and who had been killed the year Heinemann had been in Vietnam. "He probably deserved it more than I do," Heinemann said, wiping tears from his eyes.

Enchanted is an overworked word, but that night we spent an enchanted evening aboard a sampan on the River of Perfumes, which bisects Hue east-and-west. Five young singers in traditional *ao dais* serenaded us to the accompaniment of five musicians playing traditional instruments. In between songs, we recited poems to each other in English and Vietnamese. Thieu's on-the-spot translation of my love poem "Channel Fever" was twice as long as the English version I'd just recited, and sounded twice as beautiful.

"How did you do that?" I asked incredulously.

"Oh, I only understood about half of what you were saying," he replied. "But I could feel your passion. I just translated the passion."

The next day, we returned to Danang, checked into our hotel, then set off immediately for Marble Mountain, China Beach and

Hoi An. I had asked to go to Hoi An, knowing that the only road to the city would have to pass right by my old battalion command post, where I'd spent my first eight months during the war. What I hadn't counted on was that the Vietnamese might have built a new road in the ensuing twenty-three years.

Actually, it turned out to have been the Koreans who had built the new road not long after my battalion had shifted north, but that didn't really matter. What mattered was that, the moment we began heading south from China Beach, I knew we were going to miss the spot I was looking for. I tried to get Hai Hoc, general secretary of the Danang Writers' Association, to understand what I wanted. The discussion got rather heated. Hai Hoc, in fact, must have thought I was a crazy. It was clear that he thought I didn't know what I was talking about. Our afternoon in Hoi An was strained, but after another brief and heated discussion, he ordered the bus driver to take a different road north to Danang.

And there it was — or there it should have been. I knew from the locations of a mountain, a river, a stream and a bridge that the front gate of the old CP had to be right here, and behind that gate, surrounded by a high sand perimeter topped with hundreds of coils of barbed concertina wire, should have been several acres of bare sand where nothing grew or ever would grow. But where the old CP had stood, there was now a thriving village of several thousand people, all living in brick and tile homes surrounded by palm trees and banana trees and all manner of living, green things. For a moment I was uncomfortably unsure, wondering in a panic if I'd just made a fool of myself. But I couldn't be wrong. I'd spent too much time sitting on that berm, staring west at the river and the mountain beyond it. Too much had happened here.

As soon as we stopped the bus, a crowd of villagers gathered around to see the strange foreigners who'd come to visit them. I asked an old man if there were two concrete French bunkers nearby. His face lighting up, he pointed back over his shoulder and gestured for me to follow him. Fifty meters off the road, obscured by trees and the densely packed houses, stood the two bunkers. One had a house built right on top of it. The other had a house built around two sides of it. Hai Hoc smiled broadly and shook my hand. This American wasn't crazy, after all.

Twenty-three years ago, the front entrance to the old CP had passed right between those two bunkers. No other evidence remained to indicate that we Americans had ever been there — and even the bunkers had been built by the French before us. It was all gone. Every trace of our presence. The little hamlet that had cowered under the northwest corner of our wire had absorbed it all, seeming to thrive and prosper on the detritus of our passing.

Twenty-three years is a long time, Vietnam is a verdant land, and the Vietnamese are a resilient people, so it should not have startled me that they have buried our remains and built right over them. But memory is a powerful thing, and I had had no way to see what had transpired in my long absence. I was prepared for abandoned ruins like I'd seen at Phu Bai, or a vast expanse of barren sand, but I had not anticipated this, and so I was startled almost beyond words. The old man was still standing next to me. "Nice village you've got here," I managed to stammer after a long moment. "A lovely village indeed. It makes me happy to see it." And then it was me who was wiping the tears from my eyes. When I left, he was still standing there surrounded by several dozen children and young people, no doubt all of them wondering who I was.

That night we met with the Danang Writers' Association in a cramped upstairs room decorated with only a drawing of Leo Tolstoy. (In 1985, no official gathering would have been without a portrait of Ho Chi Minh, more often than not flanked by Marx and Lenin, but life in Vietnam is changing rapidly.) "Our hair is gray," Ngan Vin Le began, "but in writing, forty is the age of youth. I am glad we did not meet as soldiers. Each of us was threatened by the war, but each of us survived. Now it is our duty as writers to arouse the conscience of the people of the world in the cause of peace."

A special rapport rapidly and visibly developed between Le and Caputo. Both men had been platoon commanders in the Danang area, had perhaps even been direct adversaries. And when Le described a poem he had once written about sheltering a dying comrade from the rain, novelist Caputo blurted out, "I've only written three poems in my entire life, but one of them was about an incident exactly like that!"

"I was an army medic," said Thai Ba Loi, 45, who had been a member of Le's platoon. "But that doesn't mean I didn't use a weapon. I wasn't a very good marksman, but once I actually managed to bring down an American helicopter with a lucky shot. One crewman survived, but he was wounded in the stomach. He asked for water, but I couldn't give it to him because of his stomach wound. I myself performed the surgery. He was still alive when we turned him over to a unit west of here. I don't know what happened to him after that."

Then Tran Thi My Nhung recited a poem he had written only the previous year called "A Vietnamese Bidding Farewell to the Remains of an American":

> Was your plane on fire, or did you die
> of bullet wounds, or fall down exhausted?
> Just so you died in the forest, alone.
>
> Only the two of us, a woodcutter and his wife,
> dug this grave for you, burned joss sticks,
> prayed for you to rest in peace.
>
> How could we know there'd be such a meeting,
> you and I, once separated by an ocean,
> by the color of our skin, by language?
>
> But destiny bound our lives together.
> And today, by destiny's grace,
> you are finally going home.
>
> I believe your American sky
> is as blue as the sky above this country
> where you've rested twenty years.
>
> Is it too late to love each other?
> Between us now, the ocean seems so small.
> How close are our two continents.
>
> I wish a tranquil heaven for your soul,
> gemmed with twinkling stars and shining moon.
> May you rest forever in the soil of your home.

As the meeting ended, Le and Caputo embraced. "He really hugged me," Caputo said as we were leaving. "I don't think he was faking that. He really meant it."

In Haiphong, Hue and Danang, we had stayed in regular commercial hotels—not exactly four-star accommodations, but comfortable enough. In Ho Chi Minh City, however, we found ourselves once again in a government guest house several miles from the center of town. It's a beautiful and stately complex of buildings, really, but rather isolated. Heinemann immediately dubbed it the

"Dipstick Hilton." Thieu, a northerner who had been eagerly awaiting this rare visit to the city of culture, sin and adventure, shook his head. "This is a very sad place," he said, looking around at the complex.

All sorts of tensions had been flowing beneath the surface of this entire trip. Vietnam is still trying to find its way to the future, and there is keen competition among the so-called reformers, loosely centered around Foreign Minister Nguyen Co Thach, who wants to liberalize Vietnam's political and economic systems, and the hard-line ideologues, centered around the Interior Ministry, who want to stick strictly to the revolutionary vision that sustained them through three decades of war. For the past six or seven years, the reformers have been in the ascendancy, and the effects of their influence can be seen in everything from Le Luu's popular and unflattering novel (which would never have been published as late as 1984), to the increase since 1985 in foreign-made goods in the markets of Hanoi, to the glittering Australian-built floating hotel on the banks of the Saigon River.

But since early 1990, the ideologues have begun to reassert themselves, thanks to the Bush Administration's abandonment of the terms for normalization of relations explicitly laid down by Reagan, which has left Foreign Minister Thach with nothing to show for his withdrawal of Vietnamese troops from Cambodia but a resurgence of the genocidal Khmer Rouge, and to the remarkable chain of events sweeping Eastern Europe, which the ideologues seem firmly to believe was engineered by the Central Intelligence Agency. Only two months before our arrival, Interior police detained for three weeks, and then deported, U.S. businessman Michael Morrow, a longtime friend of Vietnam and a guest of the Foreign Ministry. Just days before we arrived, teacher Miriam Hershberger, a Mennonite Central Committee volunteer, was also deported, like Morrow for espionage and "attempting to destabilize Vietnam."

These and similar incidents are surface manifestations of the powerful struggle now underway for control of Vietnam, and the struggle is reflected at virtually all levels of Vietnamese society. Our conference, in fact, had originally been scheduled to take place in November 1989, but several members of the Writers' Association suggested that it had been blocked repeatedly by hard-liners in and out of the Association. The amount of press coverage we received, our audiences with Thach, Giap, and southern commander General Tran Van Tra also suggested that equally powerful people wanted our visit to be a success.

Thus Nguyen Quang Sang explained that we had been put up in Ho Chi Minh City's government guest house in order to try to minimize the chance that Interior police might try to create an "incident" involving one or more of us (much like the apparently trumped-up incidents involving Morrow and Hershberger).

But things are never simple in Vietnam. Beneath the very real ideological struggle (perhaps alongside it would be more accurate) is the ongoing struggle between northerners and southerners, which might be likened to the perpetual struggle between regions in the U.S. Northerners traveling with us suggested that what really motivated Quang, a native southerner, was a desire to impress upon the northerners that they were in the south now, this was his turf, he was in control, and this was now his show.

God only knows what was really going on—one would have to remain in Vietnam infinitely longer than I did to be able to sort it all out—but it was certainly fascinating. Meanwhile, we Americans, by now down to six (Bowen and Weigl having returned to the States on other business, Wilson having headed back up-country in search of another story), made do with what we were given.

Our first night in Ho Chi Minh City, we went to a private screening of filmmaker Sang's newest production, *The Singing River*. It is the story of an American journalist who inadvertently falls into the hands of the Viet Cong, sees the war from the other side, and comes away sympathetic to the revolution, all of which is layered over several interwoven love stories. Vietnamese film production is extremely crude by U.S. standards; the Vietnamese lack sophisticated equipment, technical expertise, and money. And their films, like the people themselves, are overtly and unabashedly sentimental.

Still, the central character in this Vietnamese film is an American (played by a French-Vietnamese actor named Robert Hai, 51), and though he is not quite convincing, Sang has made a serious attempt to portray Americans as real people with depth and substance, something I have yet to see Americans do with Vietnamese in our films about the war. (During Sang's 1989 visit to the

U.S., he spent many hours interviewing U.S. veterans, attempting to understand them so that he could portray them as something more than "cogs in the U.S. war machine.")

On the way back to the guest house, children's writer Ly Lan, 33, another member of the younger generation, told me about herself: "I was just eighteen in 1975, a student in Saigon. I didn't know about the bombing and the suffering until after the war ended. During the war, all it had meant to me was foreign soldiers in my city. I didn't like them very much, so I was happy when peace came, but I was afraid of the new government. I didn't know what to expect. Still, I am Vietnamese, and I wanted to help rebuild my country." When I asked if she liked the new regime these days, she made a mildly sour face and shrugged, as if to say, "It could be better."

The next day, we drove to Tay Ninh Province for a meeting with the Tay Ninh Writers' Association. By this time, having kept to a truly grueling schedule for nearly two weeks, I was physically exhausted. The thought of yet another meeting where everyone has time to say only a sentence or two between introductions and toasts to the eternal friendship of former enemies made my eyes glaze over and my brain turn to mush. Even the cold milk sipped directly from unhusked coconuts did little to revive me, and I have little recollection of what was said at the meeting.

But I do remember lunch, as always an elaborate affair with multiple courses, because I sat next to Minh Thu, 40, a correspondent for Television Ho Chi Minh City, and "Mi Ti," as she calls herself, told me a remarkable story. Her father went north as a soldier in 1952, and she, her mother and brother never heard from him again, though her mother kept insisting that he would come back. In the late 1960s, her mother was arrested by the regime of Nguyen Van Thieu and imprisoned for four years because her husband "was a communist." During this time, she and her brother lived with relatives who told the children repeatedly that their father was dead. But on the day the war ended in 1975, there was a knock on the door, and Mi Ti answered it. There stood a man in uniform. "You are Mi Ti, aren't you?" he said. "I am your father." And then he gathered her into his arms and "cried like a baby." Pointing to her chin, Mi Ti told me, "He recognized me by this birthmark. My parents have been together ever since. They are very happy."

Driving back to Ho Chi Minh City, we stopped at the town of Trang Bang, where Heinemann and his buddies used to drink beer and shoot pool in 1967, parking their APC right in the middle of the town square. But when we arrived, there was no pool hall and no town square. Nothing looked familiar. "It was all leveled during the last days of the fighting in 1975," one of the townspeople told us as he swept his arm in a full circle. Rottmann managed to find a dozen cans of Heineken, and we stood in the dirty street drinking warm beer for awhile, then got back in the van and left.

The next day, we visited the Amerasian Transit Center, where Amerasian children await final clearance to leave for the U.S. It was positively eerie: several hundred teenagers and young adults, a disproportionate number of them Black Amerasian, stared at us as if we were their fathers. Some of them even laughlingly shouted, "Daddy!" But it wasn't funny, and one could almost touch the desperation in their voices. One boy, when asked by Caputo to describe the happiest and saddest days of his life, replied, "I have never had a happy day." Another girl, a young woman of 20 named Tran Thanh Huong who is illiterate, told us that she had been too poor to go to school, and had worked all her life as a helper on a family farm. "I want to go to America to learn English and earn money for a better life," she said, "but I don't know if I will find what I want."

All of them are hoping for a better life in the U.S. Most of them will not find it. Out of place as they have been in Vietnam, most will be even more displaced in the U.S. With no knowledge of English or of American culture, with no support network of family or friends, with doubtful prospects for being accepted either by American society at large or by the smaller society of the Vietnamese-American community, most will find menial work or no work at all, ending up at the very bottom of the heap, perhaps homeless, perhaps drawn into petty crime, drugs, and the thousand other pitfalls that await the truly helpless. What could we say to these children, who gazed at us with penetrating eyes, as if trying to see their own futures? I have seldom felt so uncomfortable in all my life. I have seldom hated the war more than I did that afternoon.

On our last night in Vietnam, the Ho Chi Minh City Writers' Association treated us to a farewell banquet aboard the *Cosevina 2*, a floating restaurant *cum* riverboat. For several hours, we cruised the Saigon River in the quiet darkness, eating crabs' legs, stuffed snails, chicken, fish and rice while drinking 33 Export beer, Coca-Cola, brandy and *lua moi*, a potent Vietnamese rice vodka. A television sat on a chair at the bow of the boat, tuned to a World Cup soccer match, and though the reception was poor, a cluster of Vietnamese — both men and women — gathered around the set to find out what had happened every time the crowd let out a roar.

"Do you have a copy in English of that poem you gave to General Giap?" asked Colonel Le Kim, a writer from Hanoi who had reappeared in Ho Chi Minh City. (I had given Giap a Vietnamese version of "Making the Children Behave.")

"Yes I do," I said. "Would you like to have it?"

"It's not for me. It's for General Giap."

"Does he read English?" I asked. (Giap had spoken only Vietnamese during our two-hour meeting in Hanoi.)

"Oh, yes," Le Kim replied with a twinkle, "very well. He liked your poem in Vietnamese, but he would like to know what it *really* says."

In all my life, I have met only two American generals: one pinned a medal on me; the other said, "Carry on, Corporal. Sergeant! Excuse me, my eyesight must be going." Now in these two weeks, I'd met seven generals. One of the greatest generals of the 20th century actually liked a poem of mine enough to send Le Kim a thousand miles to find me. Perhaps I'm being too harsh, but I have a very hard time imagining General William Westmoreland reading my poetry.

Once, in 1975, I had coffee with Congressman Edward G. Beister. It was 7:45 a.m., in his office in Langhorne, Pennsylvania, and he shaved and dressed as we talked. When he tied his tie, our meeting was over. In Vietnam, I had a two-hour audience with the foreign minister. (Just for fun, after I got home in late June, I wrote a letter to Secretary of State James Baker, asking if I could meet with him to share the substance of my discussion with his Vietnamese counterpart, Thach. Six weeks later, I received a letter from one Charles H. Twining, Director, Office of Vietnam, Laos and Cambodia, suggesting that "the most efficient means of communicating [my] assessment would be in writing.")

"The Joiner Center, and you, are well known in Hanoi," wrote Vietnam veteran and novelist John Del Vecchio a week after I received Twining's letter. "There is very definitely a public relations angle being worked by Hanoi, and your visit is very definitely a part of it." I have no doubt that such was and is true. But at least the Vietnamese are paying attention, which is more than I can say for the folks in Washington, D.C. I may have played right into the hands of a *real politik* secret Vietnamese agenda, but I went to Vietnam this time with my own agenda, and I used the Vietnamese to achieve it.

It did my heart good to walk the streets of Hue without coming under a murderous crossfire. It did my heart good to see people working the once-desolate earth along the road to Con Thien. It did my heart good to see that thriving village where once had stood a wasteland of barbed wire, sand and canvas. It did my heart good to meet men and women from the other side who survived a war and have dedicated their lives to making sense of their experience through the written word.

And for perhaps the first time in my life, I was not made to feel like the odd man out because I am a "Vietnam writer." In the U.S., I get invited to read at conferences called "Tet Plus Twenty" and "Vietnam Reconsidered," but I've never been invited to read at the Breadloaf Writers' Conference or the Geraldine R. Dodge Poetry Festival. My poems are taught in college history courses on the Vietnam war, but not in classes on contemporary American poetry. And even some of my closest and dearest friends have wondered aloud when I'm going to write a book "that isn't about Vietnam," their genuine concern for my psychological wellbeing irritatingly evident in their tone of voice.

But in Vietnam, everybody over the age of 35 is a "Vietnam writer," and for once I could feel like just one of the gang. No one thinks it odd to be writing about the war, much less its painful and lingering legacies. No one looks at you as if you are emotionally retarded. What I've done with my life and my writing makes perfectly good sense to them. They see it, as I do, as a duty and an obligation, a way of turning disaster into hope. All of us learned things that are too important to be ignored or forgotten or left behind.

And if I have failed, in the words of Ngan Vin Le, "to rouse the conscience of the people of the world in the cause of peace" (and it seems fairly certain that I have)—well, there are worse things one might fail at. And even worse ways to succeed.

MILITARY HISTORY
OF W. D. EHRHART

W. D. Ehrhart formally enlisted in the Marines on 11 April 1966, while still in high school, beginning active duty on 17 June. He graduated from basic recruit training at the Marine Corps Recruit Depot, Parris Island, South Carolina, as a private first class on 12 August and completed his basic infantry training at Camp Lejeune, North Carolina, on 12 September 1966. (While at Parris Island, he qualified as a rifle sharpshooter on 18 July 1966, subsequently qualifying as a rifle expert on 11 April 1968 and as a pistol sharpshooter on 24 April 1969.)

Assigned to the field of combat intelligence, Ehrhart spent 10 October to 15 December 1966 with Marine Air Group 26, a helicopter unit based at New River Marine Corps Air Facility, North Carolina, meanwhile completing a clerk typist course at Camp Lejeune in November 1966 and graduating first in his class from the Enlisted Basic Amphibious Intelligence School at Little Creek Amphibious Base, Norfolk, Va., in December 1966. He also completed a Marine Corps Institute combat intelligence correspondence course in December while at New River.

Before leaving for Vietnam on 9 February 1967, Ehrhart received additional combat training with the 3rd Replacement Company, Staging Battalion, Camp Pendleton, California, in January and February. Upon arrival in Vietnam, he was assigned to the 1st Battalion, 1st Marine Regiment, first as an intelligence assistant, later as assistant intelligence chief. In March 1967, he was temporarily assigned to the Sukiran Army Education Center,

Okinawa, where he graduated first in his class from a course in basic Vietnamese terminology before returning to permanent assignment.

While in Vietnam, Ehrhart participated in the following combat operations: Stone, Lafayette, Early, Canyon, Calhoun, Pike, Medina, Lancaster, Kentucky I, Kentucky II, Kentucky III, Con Thien, Newton, Osceola II, and Hue City. He was promoted to lance corporal on 1 April 1967 and to corporal on 1 July 1967.

Ehrhart was awarded the Purple Heart for wounds received during Operation Hue City, a commendation from the commanding general of the 1st Marine Division, two Presidential Unit Citations, the Navy Combat Action Ribbon, the Vietnam Service Medal with three stars, the Vietnamese Cross of Gallantry with palm, the Civil Action Meritorious Unit Citation, and the Vietnamese Campaign Medal. He completed his Vietnam tour on 28 February 1968.

Ehrhart was next assigned to the 2nd Marine Air Wing Headquarters Group at Cherry Point Marine Corps Air Station, North Carolina, from 30 March to 10 June 1968, where he was promoted to sergeant on 1 April. After a brief assignment with the Headquarters Squadron of Marine Air Group 15 based at Iwakuni Marine Corps Air Station, Japan, he was then reassigned to Marine Aerial Refueler Transport Squadron 152, Futema Marine Corps Air Facility, Okinawa, from 20 July to 30 October 1968, where he received a commanding officer's meritorious mast.

Ehrhart completed his active duty with Marine Fighter Attack Squadron 122, based alternately at Iwakuni and Cubi Point Naval Air Station, Philippines, from 31 October 1968 to 30 May 1969. While in the Philippines, he completed a field course on jungle environmental survival in February 1969.

On 10 June 1969, Ehrhart was separated from active duty, receiving the Good Conduct Medal. While on inactive reserve, he was promoted to staff sergeant on 1 July 1971. He received an honorable discharge on 10 April 1972.

INDEX

ABOUT THE AUTHOR

W. D. Ehrhart was born in 1948 in Roaring Spring, Pennsylvania, and grew up in Lewisburg and Perkasie, both also in Pennsylvania. He holds a bachelor's degree from Swarthmore College and a master's degree from the University of Illinois at Chicago. A writer by profession, he occasionally teaches at both the high school and college levels. Currently, he lives in Philadelphia, Pennsylvania, with his wife, Anne, and daughter, Leela.

Ehrhart's first published work appeared in the 1972 VVAW-sponsored anthology *Winning Hearts and Minds: War Poems by Vietnam Veterans.* Since then his prose and poetry have appeared in several hundred periodicals and anthologies in the United States as well as Australia, Britain, Czechoslovakia, France, Germany, India, Italy, Israel, the Netherlands, Nicaragua, Portugal, Spain, Vietnam, and Yugoslavia.

Ehrhart is the recipient of grants and awards from the Academy of American Poets, the Mary Roberts Rinehart Foundation, the Pennsylvania Council on the Arts, Veterans for Peace, Inc., and the Vietnam Veterans of America Foundation. He has read and lectured widely in the U.S. and abroad, and has been a Writer-in-Residence at the Washington Project for the Arts, an Isota Tucker Epps Lecturer at the Shipley School, a George A. Miller Committee Lecturer at the University of Illinois, and most recently Visiting Professor of War and Social Consequences at the William Joiner Center, University of Massachusetts at Boston.